Kids of New York

Family, Street Culture, Violence

An Autobiography

ANTHONY COLON

PAGE PUBLISHING
Conneaut Lake, PA

First originally published by Page Publishing 2023

ISBN 979-8-88793-721-2 (pbk)
ISBN 979-8-88793-730-4 (digital)

Printed in the United States of America

Introduction

I wrote this book out of dire necessity. A story that needed to be told of a young boy who grew up in the perils of the ghetto. Thrust into a life of poverty and despair. A very young child who lived day-to-day without a glimpse of where he would end up. Like many other young kids who've grown up in very rough patches as well, I, that same boy, dedicate this book to all of you. There are countless stories in the ghettos of America, which sadly include many tragedies but also many victories as well. From the darkness, one can see the light. From the many pitfalls that one may endure, one must stand up, dust oneself off, and keep moving forward. For life is the struggle, the strife, and the true understanding of oneself.

I'm not a prolific writer, scholar, or Pulitzer-prized author. As a matter of fact, this is my first attempt at writing a book—my memoir so to speak. I'm just someone who was there at the wrong place at the wrong time. I've witnessed some atrocities that no child should ever bear witness to, or any adult for that matter. I grew up in New York City in the 1970s and 1980s, throughout the most devastating and rampant years of drug abuse in the Big Apple.

Unfortunately, drugs were plentiful on the city streets. Drugs could basically be purchased openly on any street corner. Illegal drugs like heroin, cocaine, marijuana, angel dust, LSD, and sadly, the shadow of death itself, crack, were plenty available. Crack took its hold on the city and surrounding suburban communities. It was a drug like no other the world had seen before. Crackheads ravaged the city with crime. If you felt the city was bad before, it got much worse during the crack years. Murders skyrocketed. NYC became the murder capital of the good ole USA.

Like most normal kids, I played outside, watched Saturday morning cartoons, and was raised in a very religious household with ethics, morals, and respectful family values. Somewhere along the line, something went wrong, very wrong! This is my story—just one of the millions of stories in the naked city.

South Bronx…ruins
New York Post, daily news clips

Chapter 1

1. Early Years in the South Bronx

I was born in Jacobi Hospital in the South Bronx on May 12,1970. The neighborhood was a valley of death, misery, and misfortune. Drugs, gangs, crime, and despair were present in everyday life. The South Bronx was the mecca of human deprivation in America. This was my birthplace. My father and mother both migrated from Puerto Rico. They met in the city and began a romance that produced the author of this narrative. They were young and in love. Poor and lacking in a formal education, they struggled to make ends meet. Most people living in this neighborhood were going through the same hardships. My parents broke up when I was very young. My father had some issues to resolve. He had a drinking problem. My father died soon after at the tender age of eighteen.

Later on, Mom met and married my stepfather, Antonio. He raised me as one of his own with his firstborn son, Edward. We were raised as brothers in a tight-knit family. To this day, I love them both dearly. We moved to Springfield, Massachusetts, seeking a better quality of life, and it was, well at least for a while.

Oftentimes, I was sent to stay with my grandmother in the Bronx. The years were 1973–1976. My grandmother lived on Westchester Avenue. She lived in a basement apartment. It was dark, dingy, with rodents, and roach infested. Most buildings in the South Bronx at that time were run down by slumlords. Nevertheless, I really enjoyed playing in the lobby and yard of the building. I constantly watched the loud airplanes fly overhead and made buzzing sounds with my mouth as they passed by. I also made train sounds as well after riding the subway, which I called the Le Le.

Grandma often bought me acappurias. Acappurias were a Puerto Rican delicacy made of plantains filled with meat. They were absolutely delicious. She also bought me limbes. Limbes are multiflavored ices such as guayaba, coconut, pineapple, etc. We also drank piraguas, which were slushy drinks. I loved spending time with Grandma. She was awesome. We walked through the Hunts Point area, going in and out of mom-and-pop stores. We went grocery shopping at the local supermarket. Occasionally, we'd get slices and a soda at the local pizzeria. A slice was only fifty cents. Grandma loved pizza. Sadly, she ate pizza the night she passed away.

One afternoon, Grandma and I took a subway ride into Brooklyn to visit my aunt Juanita. We boarded the 2 Train at Freeman Avenue station in the Bronx and then transferred to the J train at the Delancey Street station in Manhattan. We rode over the Williamsburg Bridge into Brooklyn. I gazed at all the buildings as we crossed the mighty East River. I distinctly remember the Ortiz funeral sign as we came off the bridge into the borough of Brooklyn. We exited the train at the Flushing Avenue stop a few minutes later. We then proceeded to walk to the housing projects on Humboldt Avenue. My aunt and her kids lived there. I played outside with my cousins Michelle, Raymond, and Debbie until nightfall. We played double Dutch, jacks, hopscotch, and a variety of other street games. After dinner, we watched the *Wizard of Oz* on TV. It was my first time seeing this movie. I was truly mesmerized and captivated by the film. A true Hollywood classic.

During the day, back in the Bronx, I watched cartoons such as *Mr. Magoo*, *Abbott and Costello*, *The Flintstones*, *The Fantastic Four*, *Spiderman*, etc. Grandma made me farina. It was a spanish-flavored oatmeal. She also made arroz con leche, which was milk with rice, and an herbal drink called mavi. I loved this special time with Grandma. Grandma was very religious and prayed while wearing a headpiece. She always had her Bible by her bedside. She was very affectionate and loving, but at times when I was very rowdy and naughty, she would punish me. She would crack me with her thick sandals or had me kneel on rice and pray to God for forgiveness. "Incate," she said, which meant "kneel and pray."

In the afternoons, I went outside and played with cap guns, army men, big wheels, go-karts, cap rockets, parachute men, wooden airplanes, and Tonka trucks.

I stayed up late at night and watched TV. I watched *Chiller* and *Fright Night*. My uncle Paul, a.k.a. Indio, also lived with Grandma. My uncle Paul had many trophies for boxing and track. He also had some strange items around the house, including a stuffed leopard head with gleaming eyes and protruding fangs, which he kept on a bookshelf. Every time I watched scary movies, I would glance over my shoulder and see this hideous creature staring back at me. It was frightening. Also at night, during the witching hour, the critters came out to play. Remember, this was the South Bronx in the 1970s. Buildings were in disrepair and decaying due to the slumlords who didn't give a damn about their tenants. It was a very scary time for me. The bugs and vermin played at night—yup, giant roaches, water bugs, centipedes, millipedes, and other scary critters. The mice also joined the party.

Man! I was always ready with a broom or sandals. I was mortified. When I turned on the kitchen light, the roaches scattered. There were thousands. They were on the floor, walls, and cupboards. I was appalled and disgusted. Grandma had Roach Motels everywhere, but they didn't work too well. She also used chinese chalk, which never worked. The roaches' antennae stuck up like radar while scavenging for food. Those nasty, disgusting little runts. Yuck, I couldn't stand them. The bathroom was even worse. It was the valley of death. That was where the water bugs hung out. I turned on the hot water and tried to kill as many as possible. Taking a shower was a nightmare. Eventually, even though the heat was unbearable in the summer nights of the 1970s, I'd get sleepy and crash. I always fell asleep on Grandma's bed. She always kept her dentures in a drinking glass on the nightstand alongside her Coke bottle glasses. I always drifted off to the sound of the box fan in the window and the sound of the voices permeating from the streets. Yup!

2. The Big Move to Springfield, 1973

My earliest childhood recollection was moving to Springfield, Massachusetts, on a cold Christmas night in 1973. I fondly remember the Christmas lights glittering in the windows of all the houses we drove past on our journey to our new home. I was three years old, a very young child, but those images are forever etched in my memory.

We moved to a building on Main Street in the downtown area of Springfield. We lived on the third floor. My mom bathed me in the sink. I loved that. Mom played games with me and fed me. She tickled me and hugged me constantly. She was a very loving and caring mother. Dad and Edward lived with us as well. We were together for the first time as a family. However, Grandma and my uncle Paul still lived in New York. From time to time, I spent time with them back in the Bronx.

The Springfield years were very important in shaping my early thinking and behavior. It was the opposite of the Bronx, which was very crowded, loud, and crime-ridden. There was no hustle and bustle in a small town like Springfield. It was a slow and methodical place. The schools were very good, and teachers really helped and guided students. Nature was very prevalent in a small town like Springfield. It had lots of houses, trees, gardens, and lakes. The people were down-to-earth and were very plain and simple. Yet Springfield was a migrating point for many Puerto Ricans moving north from New York City.

We left the South Bronx because our building was condemned, and besides that, Mom wanted a better and more prosperous life for her family. Unfortunately, this was not going to be the case. Nope.

3. Bruce Lee's Death, 1973

Bruce Lee died on July 20, 1973. I was too young to remember the day that Bruce Lee passed away, but I recall hearing all types of fascinating stories about his death throughout the 1970s, like the time he fought a hundred men and beat them all but fell to the old

4

master's death touch or how he was poisoned by the Chinese mafia or how he trained so much and so hard that it caused him to have a brain tumor. The tales were endless. But one thing was certain: Bruce Lee made his mark on the world and transformed the lives of millions around the globe. People from all walks of life started learning martial arts due to his undeniable talent and inspiration. Bruce Lee, the master. Yup.

4. Julissa and Maribel, 1974

Shortly after arriving to Springfield, my dad decided to bring his two daughters from another relationship into our home. (At that time, it was only Mom, Dad, Edward, and me.) Dad felt guilty that they were so far away. They both lived in Stamford, Connecticut. He tried his best to be a good father. My two stepsisters' names were Julissa, a.k.a. Ichy, and Maribel. We were the Puerto Rican version of the Brady Bunch.

In the beginning, everything was great. I was very happy to have sisters and, of course, a brother. We all played together, watched TV together, ate dinner together, had family outings together. Heck, we did everything together. Mom took a beautiful family picture of the four of us siblings. I still have a copy of this picture till this day.

I loved my new family, but Mom was feeling overworked and overwhelmed. She was young and inexperienced. She wasn't used to taking care of four very young and needy children. It was wreaking havoc on her nerves. Also, the fact that my siblings were from my dad's previous marriage, Mom really cared and loved them, but she was very jealous of my dad. She was finding it very hard to control her emotions. Many arguments erupted between because of the situation.

Dad made the difficult decision to have his daughters return and stay with his aunt and uncle in Stamford, Connecticut. Permanently. I didn't understand why they were gone. I was very upset. "Where are my sisters?" I cried. We traveled across state lines ever so often to visit them, but I always felt a sense of deep sadness every time we came back home without them. Eventually, they moved to Puerto

Rico. My sisters were gone forever, but I still had something to look forward to though: my brother Edward. Yup!

5. Street Fight Mom, 1974

My earliest memory of my parents involved a street altercation would go as far back as 1974. We lived in a housing community back then. My parents were very much in love, but there was one major problem: Mom was extremely jealous. Not good. Not good at all. My parents had some friends over for dinner one night. One of the friends, a young female, made a pass at my dad. Mom found out. The shit hit the fan.

One afternoon, shortly after the incident, Edward and I were playing outside in the backyard. The female who precariously made a pass at my dad had the audacity to pass by our house and whisper some derogatory comments under her breath. She wore one of those head wraps like Anita from the *West Side Story*. Mom was livid and asked Edward, "What did she say?" My brother replied, "Mom, she called you a *cabrona*!" This was a major insult for Puerto Ricans. It implied that your spouse or lover was sleeping around behind your back. It also signified that you had horns and that your so-called loving partner was deceptive and sticking it to you.

I'll never forget what happened next. Mom flew into a rage. She quickly threw Vaseline on her face and then tied her hair up in a knot, tightened her jeans, and set off to meet Mrs. Flirtatious. Mom followed the woman into the laundry room. My brother and I waited in the backyard for a few minutes. Dad was in the house, totally unaware of what was happening. Suddenly, the young lady stormed out of the laundry room with a large gaping wide hole in her head. Blood was gushing out. She was bleeding profusely from her wound as she screamed at the top of her lungs. The lady ran off with my mother in hot pursuit. Mom returned to the yard a few seconds later with blood all over her hands. Mom, in all her rage, had slammed the woman's head into the corner of a washing machine. I started crying, and my brother freaked out.

The lady came back with a knife to confront Mom. By that time, Mom was talking to Dad. As the young lady approached with a knife in her hand, Mom, in self-defense, picked up one of those green caterpillar buggy toys to use as a weapon. Mom swung the toy at the lady as she lunged with the knife. Dad quickly intervened and calmed both women down.

Soon after, the woman's husband came over to our house and spoke with Dad. They spoke for a while, very calmly and gentlemanly you might say. The opposite of the women. They both shook hands at the end of the conversation, and the woman's husband left. Later that evening, there was a loud thunderstorm. The rain was pouring like cats and dogs. We heard a loud thump at the door. My dad looked through the peephole. My brother and I peeked through the window. It was the fuzz, better known as the police. To my dismay, Dad pulled out his .45 caliber handgun and yelled at us to go upstairs. He didn't have to tell us twice. No sirree! We both scattered like bats out of hell and dived under our beds like a scene out of *Scooby Doo*. We took a quick glance outside from the upstairs window and saw cops everywhere with their guns drawn. *Holy moly!* I thought. The thunderstorms were very violent and nerve-racking. It was the perfect setting for the drama that was unfolding before us.

Moments later, we came down, and the police were inside. My mom was giving a statement and showing off some of her battle scars from the fight. My dad was also talking with the police. Things had calmed down. *Where's Dad's gun?* I wondered. *He must have hidden it.* Anyway, everything turned out well. Thank goodness! Yup.

6. The First Fire, 1975

In 1975, our family moved to a small four-floor building in a rundown area of town. My parents held down good jobs but still didn't make enough money to buy a house, so they had to make do with the earnings they made at the time. It was a high-crime area with many thefts and burglaries. There were two abandoned lots on the premises, one on each side of the building.

My brother Edward and I played daily in these lots, which were filled with worn-out rubber car tires, cardboard boxes, stinky mattresses, abandoned cars, run-down furniture, and broken-down appliances including old refrigerators. The old fridges had doors with latches on the outside. These old refrigerators were a death trap. If you went inside the fridge and the door latch locked behind you, you eventually suffocated. There were many cases in the 1970s of kids turning up dead several days later inside the old appliances. We played inside these death chambers several times but were fortunate enough to come out unscathed. Luckily for us.

During these early years, my dad bought an old projector camera for family fun and entertainment. The type with the reel-to-reel tapes. He played old films on it. I loved when he played cartoons. My favorite was *Woody Woodpecker*. The camera was supercool. Our family had many good times with it. My brother and I loved playing with our toys. We had race car tracks (Tyco), army men, cowboys and Indians, Batman and Robin action figures, plastic machine guns (SWAT), slingshots, bow and arrows, Evel Knievel plastic motorcycles, *Star Trek* action figures (Captain Kirk and Spock), *Godzilla* figures, Hot Wheels and Matchbox cars, boardgames, etc.

We got along really well, but at times, he didn't feel like playing, so I learned to improvise and played alone. Ha ha, with my imaginary friend. I had a very creative and vivid imagination. My brother, Edwin, was three years older than me. He really enjoyed watching TV shows like *The Munsters*, *The Addams Family*, *The Six Million Dollar Man*, *The Incredible Hulk*, *Get Smart*, *The Brady Bunch*, *The Partridge Family*, *Starsky & Hutch*, *Baretta*, etc.

The apartment we lived in was freezing in the winter. It was run-down. We tried staying warm by using electrical space heaters. They were cheap, flimsy, and poorly made—a safety hazard and definitely a fire risk. You had to be very careful when using them, making sure they were not too close to the beds, so that in turn, the blankets wouldn't ignite. We also used the gas stove as a heater. These methods of heating up the home were very dangerous. One night in the dead of winter as we all were sleeping, a large commotion woke us up.

People in the building were yelling out loud. I could hear glass shattering. It was very dark. We tried flipping on the light switch, but nothing happened. The lights had gone out. *What the hell is going on!* I thought in a panic. Then all of a sudden, you could feel the heat and smell the smoke in the apartment. My dad yelled, "Everybody out! *Fuego, fuego, fuego,* fire!" The fire alarm was not working, so we had to make our way through the dark hallways.

I saw a flicker of light. "The lights are back on!" I shouted. As I looked up, I saw the flames shoot down the stairs from the fourth floor. The sensation of heat was tremendous. The odor of burning wood, furniture, and everything else under the sun was quite frightening. I heard the sound of crackling flames and electrical wires shooting sparks, which was very terrifying. In a rush, we hurriedly tried making our way out of the burning building. We ran for our lives as fast as we could.

As we exited the tenements, we did our best to avoid the debris that was raining down over our heads. We didn't have coats, clothes, or shoes on. We were all in pajamas. The street was full of people and fire trucks. All the families watched in shock as their building burned down. Ambulances attended to the injured. The Red Cross was present as well and helped the homeless families with clothing and shelter. It was freezing cold outside, and warm blankets were given out to all the victims of the fire. Watching our home go down in a ball of fire was heartbreaking. Yup.

7. Bruce Lee Bully, 1975

My first encounter with a bully was in 1975. The bully's name was George. We used to ride the yellow school bus together. Bruce Lee fever was rampant back then. *The Green Hornet* show played constantly on television. Bruce Lee's movies—*Enter the Dragon, Chinese Connection, The Big Boss,* and *Return of the Dragon*—played in the theaters. Bruce Lee's movies lit everyone's fire. Kids acted silly, pretending to know martial arts and made funny sounds and so on. Kung fu fever was loose.

George was a Bruce Lee fanatic but also a bully. He would go around smacking and tormenting kids on the bus. Unfortunately, there was no bus monitor at the time. For some reason, don't ask me why, he would never bother me. One day, while carrying on like a fool, he started messing around with a quiet kid named Henry. A huge mistake. Henry wore a red denim jacket with bell-bottom pants, like the outfit the Six Million Dollar Man wore on the bionic man TV show. In the seventies, kids wore jean jackets, bell-bottom pants, big-collar shirts, and Buster brown shoes.

George was making his rounds bothering everyone on the bus by making mock Bruce Lee sounds, "Futah! Futah!" He tried his nonsense on Henry, but to his surprise, Henry was not having any of it. Henry jumped up from his seat and gave George the beating of his life. A real lesson in etiquette. He pummeled George with his fists like a stern father disciplining his son. George was in tears, humiliated and embarrassed with his tail between his legs. The next day, George sat down quietly on the back of the bus. We were liberated from the daily persecution of King George. Henry was the bus hero for a day. Long live King Henry. Hooray! For he's a jolly good fellow!

8. The Wedding, 1975

Mom was always an independent thinker. She was hardworking and truly focused on the ideals she had set for herself. Dad was much more relaxed, but at certain times was very stubborn and strong natured. He was rather old-fashioned you might say. I was five years old and my brother was eight when our parents got married. I was paired with the flower girl. Well, I guess, I was the flower boy. Everyone was there. Our family, friends, and acquaintances were all in attendance for this joining of hearts. I had a gray polyester suit on with a red bow tie. I looked pretty sharp I must admit. I also wore some slippery pointed black shoes. They were so slick that I felt I was ice skating. Mom looked beautiful with her wedding gown, and Dad looked very handsome with his three-piece suit. My brother, Edward, looked very sharp and clean-cut as well.

My parents finally made their way down the stairs. The flower girl and I were following closely a few feet behind. As we came down from the top of the stairs, I suddenly slipped. It was due to the stupid shoes that I was wearing. Boom, boom, boom, I hit every step on the way down with the bottom of my tush. "Ouch!" I yelled out in agony. Everyone broke out in laughter. My face turned red with embarrassment. There was nowhere to hide. My demented cousins chided me for weeks after over the incident. Edward cracked silly jokes as well.

Overall, the wedding was beautiful with lots of guests, decorations, and food. I had tons of fun that joyous day. I was so happy for my parents. Getting married sealed the bond between Mom and Dad. Edward and I were now linked eternally together as family as well. Sadly, trouble was brewing, and a breakdown in our happy family was imminent.

You see, Dad was a debonair and good-looking man. He was tall, dark, and handsome. He reminded me of the character Hutch from the 1970s TV show *Starsky & Hutch*. Surely, Mom was a very lovely woman but nevertheless was extremely jealous. She wanted to know his every move. She was very possessive. Many arguments erupted between them. Cups and plates were hurled in all directions. Several broken pieces of furniture were left all over the floor after violent eruptions. Mom was drenched in tears and Dad ended up with a sad regretful look on his face.

During the mid-1970s, Mom made a valiant effort to return to school. She wanted so badly to get her GED. She started taking courses in a local community college called STCC (Springfield Technical Community College). She didn't speak English very well, but that didn't stop her. Oftentimes, I accompanied her to class. I was very proud of her, but Dad surely wasn't. I guess he felt insecure about himself. So again, fights broke out over the most trivial things. One day during a heated argument, Dad in a moment of anguish ripped up and destroyed all of Mom's beloved school books. Mom was devastated. She cried and cried. It was a very sad moment for both of us. Yup!

9. Fishing with Dad, 1975

One of my fondest memories growing up was going fishing with Dad. We always went fishing at Forest Park on Sunday afternoons. We got up bright and early and prepared our fishing poles for the day. Well, actually, my brother Edward and I used a tin can or a stick with a bit of string and a hook attached to the end of it. Dad always had the cool, sleek fishing pole.

We drove deep into the forest with our family car, which was usually a Pinto or some other seventies joint. Mom tagged along reluctantly. Once we reached our destination, we went scavenging for earthworms. Mom, like most women, was deathly afraid of worms, snakes, shrubs, termites, centipedes, millipedes, and all other creepy crawlers. We dug up tons of worms. The worms slithered from side to side, fighting vehemently trying to avoid capture, but it was to no avail, and into the bucket they went. We then ran down to where Dad was sitting by the lake and merrily showed him our stash. He grinned from ear to ear and said, "Good work, boys!" We smiled back. Now it was time to place the worm on the hook. *Ouch, poor worm!* I thought. But it had to be done.

So anyway, I stuck this poor creature onto this jagged hook. It squirmed violently as I jabbed repeatedly at its head with the sharp point. I tried doing it as quickly as possible so that in turn, it wouldn't suffer so. Once I accomplished the menial task, it was on to fishing. We added the bobbles to the fishing lines to let us know when the fish were nibbling or biting. Dad gave us a couple of pointers. Edward and I listened intently. We wanted fish real bad. There were trout, pumpkin, bass, and all other types of fish in the lake. We had to get some! Well, at least one. We couldn't go home empty-handed. So we tossed the hooks into the water and laid our tin cans on the ground. We just waited, waited, and waited some more. It was very peaceful in the forest. You could hear the birds rustling and chirping in the trees. It was a very calming atmosphere.

After a while, my brother and I started getting restless, so we started fooling around. We made all kinds of noises and started hussing and fussing. "Shh!" Dad whispered as he waved for us. Edward and I took a closer look. We saw the fish gathering underneath. A few of them came closer to the surface, trying to devour the worm. "Be still!" Dad said softly. "Be patient." So we waited some more. Then to my excitement, the bobble moved again and again. At that moment, my primary urge was to yank the fish out of the water. Dad said, "Slow, slow, reel him in real slow." I did what he told me. The fish started biting on the worm harder. I could now see the fish coming to the surface. He was hooked! He started splashing and flapping, but he was mine. I kept reeling him in bit by bit. And voila, what do you know, out of the water! Dad scooped him up and threw him into a bucket.

The rest of the day went by this way. All of us caught plenty of fish. Mom was a happy spectator. It was an eventful day. We left at dusk with our buckets full of fish. Soon, our bellies would be full too. We headed home, and soon after, Mom fried up the fish with a side of french fries. Delicious. Yum, yum. Fishing with Dad. Yup!

10. Saturday Morning Cartoons, 1975

The influence of television on children in the 1970s was astronomical. Children were constantly bombarded with TV commercials for toys, cereals, clothing, candy, etc. The highly influential commercials mostly aired on Saturday mornings. This was prime time for viewing by children. Every channel played them. Networks such as ABC, NBC, CBS, WOR channel 9, WPIX channel 11, WNEW channel 5, etc. By 5:00 a.m., the kids were glued to their TV sets, watching classic cartoons and shows such as *Bugs Bunny and Looney Tunes, Super Friends, The Herculoids, Space Ghost, Battle of the Planets, Mighty Mouse, Deputy Dawg, Captain Caveman, Underdog, Hong Kong Phooey, Scooby Doo, Jabberjaw, Tom and Jerry, Jonny Quest, Fat Albert, Speed Buggy, Laff-A-Lympics, Tennessee Tuxedo,* Muttley, Blue Falcon, *Woody Woodpecker, The Yogi Bear Show, Harlem Globetrotters, The Flintstones, Josie and the Pussycats, The Jetsons, Spiderman, Speed Racer,* and *Schoolhouse Rock.* A major percentage of the cartoons were produced by the team of Hanna-Barbera, juggernauts in the world of animation.

In the early afternoon, *Shazam, Bigfoot and Wildboy, Land of the Lost, Mutual of Omaha's Wild Kingdom*, ABC's *Wide World of Sports, Soul Train, Dance Fever, Solid Gold, American Bandstand, The Munsters, The Addams Family*, and *The Little Rascals* came on. Throughout the afternoon, classic movies aired including but not limited to *King Kong, Godzilla, Mighty Joe Young, Tarzan* (Johnny Weissmuller), *The Lone Ranger, Abbott and Costello, Laurel and Hardy, The Three Stooges, Buck Rogers, Flash Gordon, The Dirty Dozen, Death Wish, Dirty Harry, The Bridge on the River Kwai, The Taking of Pelham One Two Three, The West Side Story, Dog Day Afternoon*, etc.

Later in the evening, we watched *The Honeymooners, The Benny Hill Show, The Love Boat, Fantasy Island, Eight Is Enough, CHiPS, Star Trek, The Twilight Zone, The Six Million Dollar Man, The Incredible Hulk, Starsky & Hutch, S.W.A.T., Baretta, The Streets of San Francisco, The Rookies*, Grizzly Addams, *B.J. and the Bear, Charlie's Angels, Three's Company, I Love Lucy, Diff'rent Strokes, Happy Days, Laverne & Shirley, Good Times, All in the Family, The Jeffersons, The Facts of Life, Mork & Mindy, The Outer Limits, Tales from the Darkside, Bonanza, The Wild West, Kung Fu*, etc. Our biggest worries back then were the horizontal and vertical controls going out of whack and watching the drama unfold during one of our favorite shows, only to be left hanging with "To be continued" ending. Educational programs were also popular such as the following: *Captain Kangaroo, Sesame Street, Villa Alegre, Mister Rogers' Neighborhood, Electric Kingdom, Zoom, The Magic Garden, New Zoo Revue, The Great Space Coaster, Puff the Magic Dragon, Davey and Goliath, Sid and Marty Kroft*, etc.

We also indulged in late-night TV. Chiller and Fright Night showcased all kinds of horror films. They played on channel 9 and 11. The *Million Dollar Movie* and the *Big Apple* movie aired on channel 9 and 5, respectively. Great television and great times. By the way, TV soap operas were utterly *boring*! Well, at least in my opinion. *General Hospital, All My Children, The Young and the Restless, One Life to Live, As the World Turns, Guiding Light, Days of Our Lives*, etc.

Reruns were playing on TV throughout the 1970s on a regular basis of the shows *Gilligan's Island, Get Smart, Mission Impossible, The Brady Bunch, I Dream of Jeannie, Bewitched, My Three Sons, The Odd*

Couple, The Saint, Barney Miller, Taxi, The Avengers, Dark Shadows, etc. *Schoolhouse Rock* taught many kids through the joy of song and music. "Conjunction Junction What's Your Function," "I'm Just a Bill on Capitol Hill," "A Noun Is a Person, a Place, or a Thing"— These were some of the infectious lines to the melodies that still resonate in my head till this day. There were plenty of talk shows in the 1970s: Merv Griffin, Dinah Shore, Dick Cavett, Mike Douglas, and Phil Donahue, then later on, Oprah Winfrey, Jenny Jones, Morton Downey, Richard Bey, Ricki Lake, Maury Povich, and Jerry Springer hit the scene. Family shows such as *In Search Of…, That's Incredible!, Real People, Dance Fever, Candid Camera, Hee Haw, The Gong Show,* and *Sha Na Na* ruled the airwaves. Game shows were popular too— *The Price Is Right, Card Sharks, Hollywood Squares, Wheel of Fortune, The $100,000 Pyramid, The Dating Game, The Newlywed Game, Family Feud, Let's Make a Deal, Jeopardy!,* etc.

Cable TV shot to prominence in the early 1980s. WHT was viewed by the masses. The latest films played every night. Nightcap for adults drew in the curious. Most kids tried getting a peep at this program. HBO and Cinemax made their debut a few years later. Yup.

11. Drive-In Theater, 1975 (Complete)

The first few years in Springfield were great. Dad worked for the city. He worked in the sanitation department, and Mom worked as a nurse in the hospital. Mom usually worked until midnights. To pass the time, Dad often took me and my brother, Edward, to the local movie theater. We watched many classic movies such as *Walking Tall, The Three Musketeers, Escape to Witch Mountain, The Shaggy D.A., Dirty Harry,* etc. We always bought popcorn and soda at the concession stand. It was awesome. We went to the theater at least once a week. This was during regular weeknights. It was such much fun.

On the weekends, the whole family would go to the drive-in theater. It was only five dollars for a carload of people. The drive-in theater played three of four movies all night long. Mostly B movies— horror, sci-fi, action, and martial arts films. Second-rate, low-budget films. They were supercool. We saw the likes of *Dracula*, *The Brides of Dracula*, *The Incredible Melting Man*, *The Food of the Gods*, *Kingdom of the Spiders*, *The Swarm*, *The Hills Have Eyes*, *Jaws*, *Empire of the Ants*, *Death Wish*, *Attack of the Killer Tomatoes*, *The Amityville Horror*, *Inframan*, etc.

It was pizza time after the movie. We always went to a local pizzeria called Antonio's Grinders. Dad always bought a large sicilian pie with everything on it. It was so darn good. We chomped down on several slices. *Yummy!* I thought in sheer delight. I was fast asleep on the drive back home. When we arrived, Dad carried me up the stairs on his shoulders. I was awake by then, but I still pretended to be asleep. I loved it when he carried me. From the corner of my eye, I could see that my brother was totally annoyed with my antics.

On one particular Thanksgiving night, our family decided to go the local drive-in theater. It was a family affair. The newspaper advertised some cartoons that were playing that night. Our family had watched the *Bambi* and *Fantasia* movies at the drive-in theater weeks earlier. We were excited about going again. Many of my relatives had gathered, which included my loving and very religious grandmother, aunts, uncles, cousins, parents, and my brother and I.

There were four cars in our group. Every vehicle was full to capacity. We approached the movie theater's marquee, which read "Playing Now: Fritz the Cat." Edward and I thought it must be *Felix the Cat*. Most local drive-in theaters usually ran out of letters and had to improvise on their spelling. We surely thought this must be the case. We all paid the five-dollar entrance fee per car. Prices were dirt cheap back then. A total of twenty dollars. So in we went, one car after the next. The kids were all screaming, "Yeah, *muñequitos!*" which translated from Spanish means "cartoons."

We arrived early, so we were able to find really good parking spots right up in front of the screen. Dad put the speaker from the outside stand in the car and latched it to the door. The drive-in started playing upcoming attractions. We had a few minutes to run around and go to the bathroom and then pick up snacks from the concession stand. All the kids jumped out of the cars and went berserk in a frenzied rush before the movie started to snack up on popcorn, candy, hotdogs, ice cream, burgers, and soda. Once we were all situated and comfy in the car, the movie played.

Blankets were placed on top of the cars. The kids got a better view of the movie from this position. The adults watched the movie from inside the vehicles. *Fritz the Cat*, the animated movie, started. The first scene took place on a bus. It was full of rats. The bus driver was also a rat. All of a sudden, the bus driver whipped out his privates and then started pleasing himself. Some female rats dressed up in women's clothing started stripping. They all exposed their breasts and started screaming and hollering on the bus.

It was a very crazy and disturbing scene. Well, at least for our parents. It was an XXX-rated movie. All the kids were loving it though! We screamed and cheered! Yeah! My poor grandma almost passed out. Our embarrassed parents quickly whizzed us out of the drive-in theater while Grandma prayed under her breath. Poor Grandma. Funny times. Funny memories. Yup.

12. Kindergarten, 1975

I attended kindergarten in 1975. I was five years old. I learned all the basic things, like learning how to spell and add and playing all types of children's games. Our teacher read us stories from different books on a daily basis. She taught us how to carefully trace our hands on paper and then paint the outlines in many assorted colors. On other days, we drew houses with white picket fences, adorned with a beaming sun in the sky. I once drew a portrait of my loving family on a very large piece of yellow construction paper with crayons. I took it home as gift for Mom and Dad, which they both really loved. Mom stuck it on the refrigerator held aloft by several magnets for all to see.

We always had a simple lunch at noon. It was mostly sandwiches, some fruit, and a small carton of apple juice. After lunch, it was time for recess. I totally loved recess time. All the kids played in the schoolyard. I really enjoyed the jungle gyms and slides. Our teacher let us run around for a few minutes and play tag to burn off some energy. "You're it." "No, you're it!" kids shouted to one another. After playtime, we headed back inside. We were all very exhausted from the sudden outburst of fun. Our teacher gave us a final lesson of the day.

Soon it was snack time. Our very sweet and kind teacher gave every child in the class two Nilla wafer cookies with a small carton of milk. Oh, how I loved that! The tasty snack made everyone drowsy, including myself. We all laid on the floor with a towel we brought from home and took a five-minute nap. After our nap, it was time to go home. All of our parents were lined up outside. We put on our shoes and jackets. If it rained, we put on our boots and raincoats. Once outside, we were reunited with our loving parents. Sometimes, my brother picked me up from school as well. This was a very happy moment in the archives of my childhood. Yup.

13. Christmas, 1975

Christmas for me as kid was very festive. Yes, we were very poor, but very happy. We did the most we could with what very little we had. Mom worked as a nurse, and Dad worked for the city. They put in many hours for very little pay just so that my brother and I could have gifts for the holidays.

A few days before Christmas, Dad always took our family out to the countryside. It was always late at night. He always drove down extremely dark roads. When there was an area he was satisfied with, he'd stopped the car by the side of the road. Dad hurriedly jumped out of the car and ran to the back of the vehicle. He dug into the trunk and found and brandished a massive axe. "Edward, Edward!" he shouted out at my brother. "Come here now, hurry!" My brother scurried out of the back seat of the car like a frightened mouse.

Dad shined his flashlight into the darkness, which revealed a valley of beautiful pine trees. They all stood tall in formation and were very majestic. Dad scouted the area, sized them up, and then made his choice. One of them was surely going home with us on this night.

Reminiscent of two soldiers sneaking into the combat zone, my brother and Dad were very stealthy. They struck fast and with precision. They chopped down our lovely Christmas timber! Their accuracy was unmatched.

Mom and I waited in the car, keeping a lookout for other vehicles. Suddenly, Dad and Edward appeared from the darkness with the prize. They mounted the goliath tree on top of the car. It was held in place with ropes. Dad made sure that the knots were very tight. They jumped in the car eerily similar to Bo and Luke scenes from *The Dukes of Hazzard* TV show. Dad put the metal to the pedal, and off we went flying down the highway at top speed.

I always wondered about this yearly family ritual, but hey, we had a tree. I surely was a happy camper. As soon as we got home, we set up the tree. It was huge! The fresh pine scent was unforgettable. There were pine needles splayed all over the floor and an occasional acorn as well. Mom brought out the lights and adornments from the closet. Dad mounted the tree on top of a tripod. He then placed artificial snow at the bottom. My brother and I started decorating the tree. After we were done with all the trimmings, we turned on the lights. Blink, blink, blink. Wow! Astonishing! It was so beautiful, so tall. It was a very majestic tree.

In our home, we understood the real meaning of Christmas. Santa Claus was cool, but the birth of Jesus Christ was the true reason our family celebrated the holiday. A few days before December 25, our parents placed several gifts under the tree. All the gifts had name tags on them. Some gifts were for family and friends. I noticed a few were marked for Edward and I. *Hmm*, I wondered. *What could they be?* I tried sneaking a peek here and there, but my brother warned me that he'd tell Mom and Dad. "Darn!" I growled.

On Christmas Eve, my brother and I sat in front of the TV set for hours and watched classic holiday films such as *Jesus of Nazareth*, *Rudolph the Red-Nosed Reindeer*, *Frosty the Snowman*, *Santa Claus Is Comin' to Town*, *A Charlie Brown Christmas*, *The Scrooge (A Christmas Carol)*, *'Twas the Night Before Christmas*, *March of the Wooden Soldiers* starring Laurel and Hardy, *Miracle on 34th Street* starring Natalie Wood, and many other great films. Mom baked a cake with muffins and made hot chocolate with marshmallows as well. It was a joyous time.

On Christmas morning, Edward and I made breakfast in bed for Mom and Dad—pancakes, a side of bacon, scrambled eggs, toast with butter, and coffee. They were very surprised and happy. They eagerly ate their breakfast with appreciation. After breakfast my parents said "Thank you" and smiled. That was our cue. We rushed to the tree and hastily grabbed our gifts. We tore the wrappings off the gifts without regards to the mess we'd make. We were so excited, just what we always wanted. Christmas memories. Yup.

14. The Bull, 1976

During the summer months of the mid-1970s, our family spent plenty of time at the Big E. The Big E was a huge carnival that included a rodeo. It was known in the New England states as the Big East. It took place in West Springfield, Massachusetts. There was a wide array of food at the festival. All types of snacks and delicacies and all sorts of refreshments were available. They had many rides, such as roller coasters, the hammer, a Ferris wheel, etc. But the biggest attraction was the rodeo. It was amazing to watch the cowboys riding the broncos. I also enjoyed watching the clowns lassoing the horses and young bulls.

My brother and I loved candy apples and cotton candy. We also chowed down on popcorn, corn on the cob, and hotdogs with a cold soda to wash it all down. This was a very joyous time for our family. On one such great summer day, we started leaving the carnival to head home. We began exiting the carnival and heading toward the parking lot, and through the corner of my eye, I could see a bull being walked through the crowd tied by a rope by a bunch of cowboys. *How crazy!* I thought.

All of a sudden, there was a roar in the crowd, and people started running in all directions. *What's going on?* I wondered. My brother and parents started fleeing. Unfortunately, I was too far to catch up with them. My parents started yelling, "Run, run, run!" and "Corre, Bially, corre!" and boy, did I run. At that moment, I saw the bull charge toward an old woman. The bull rammed his horns into the poor woman's back as she flew up in the air. I was in shock. The bull's handlers tried recapturing the beast.

Suddenly, the bull turned and started running in my direction. By that time, everyone had disappeared, except for my parents, who kept yelling at me from a distance to run. The bull took notice of me and charged in my direction. I remember watching cartoons where the character faced moments like this, but this was no cartoon, and here I was facing my dilemma. As the bull approached, in my moment of despair, I jumped onto an RV trailer. The bull circled the RV as I screamed at the top of my lungs. It was like a scene out of *Jaws*, except that it took place on dry land. My parents were terrified. The handlers finally got control of the massive beast.

My parents had to console me and persuade me to come down from the RV. I was traumatized and in tears and never wanted to return to the Big E, the stuff of nightmares! Yup!

15. School Play, 1976

When I was six years old, I attended the William DeBerry Elementary School in the suburbs of Springfield, Massachusetts. I was in the first grade. I had a mild speech impediment. I had difficulty pronouncing words clearly. An old lady of African American descent was my speech therapist. She was lovingly referred to as Mrs. May. She was extremely kind and caring and took her time working with me. I spent many hours in her office practicing vocal patterns and pronunciation. Day after day, I practiced reciting several words and phrases under her gentle guidance. Thursday, thimble, chair, cherry, sunshine, etc., learning to speak properly and with clarity. With time, my speech problem slowly but surely improved.

As I developed confidence in my speech, I was allowed to participate in several school events. In one play, I played a tree. All I did was stand there motionless. I had no lines to read and no script to memorize. Easy as can be. My part was to just stand there and stare at the crowd. My classmates and I rehearsed for several weeks, and finally, the day of the show had arrived. The play started as planned. Several nervous kids, including myself, kept peeking through the curtains. We all tried to get a glimpse of the crowd, looking for our loved ones in the sea of spectators. After a few peeks, I located where my parents were seated. Now, I was more nervous than ever. Our group was next, and we all took our positions as the curtains were raised. We performed to the delight of our loving parents. My mom and dad embraced each other as they smiled and waved at me. I was so happy. It was one of the most joyous memorable moments of my young life. Yup.

16. Jaws, 1976

My beach-going experience changed dramatically in 1976. It was due to one movie and one movie only: the masterpiece horror film christened *Jaws*. Tun, tun, tun, tun, tun, tun was the terrifying music soundtrack that accompanied it. *Jaws* horrified beachgoers all over the world. This movie really scared the bejesus out of me. It was like no other kind of film. It was incredibly realistic and terrifying at the same time. I couldn't go into the water at the beach anymore without the fear of a giant killer shark swallowing me whole. I was even scared of taking a bath at home, thinking that a shark could be lurking at the bottom of the tub.

The performances from actors Roy Scheider, Richard Dreyfuss, and Robert Shaw were electrifying. Their on-screen chemistry on the film was magnetic. The scene where Quint (Robert Shaw) was swallowed whole by a twenty-five-foot Great White Shark was the stuff of nightmares. Even today, I would still be weary of dark waters. Other good films such as *Orca* had been released since then, but *Jaws* stood alone and was a true masterpiece that will stand the test of time. Make sure to catch it (forgive the pun) if you haven't seen it, *Jaws*.

17. Amusement Parks, 1976

One of the most joyous times for me as a kid was going to the amusement park. Our family frequented Mountain Park. It was located in Holyoke, Massachusetts. They had a great wooden roller-coaster. It was my first experience with coasters. It was very terrifying but, at the same time, an exhilarating experience. My brother and I loved going to the haunted house. He always spooked me at the moment that the haunted car ride slammed through the rickety door entering into the attraction. He tapped me over the shoulder every time a haunt appeared. "Boo!" he whispered. The haunted house was very creepy with devilish sound effects. Every turn revealed some ghoulish monsters accompanied by a loud buzzing horn.

I really enjoyed the teacups. It was more of a kids' ride. It spun in circles at a frenetic pace, causing dizziness. One ride the whole family participated on was the bumping cars ride. My brother and I chased each other down. Boom, boom, boom! We both lovingly slammed our cars into one another. Mom usually spun in circles as Dad caught her off guard and crashed into her. Mom got revenge by slamming into Dad from behind. We couldn't stop laughing. We also rode the spider ride, eagle ride, swinging boat ride, elevated swings, and the spinner ride. Then there was the majestic Ferris wheel. I wasn't very fond of this attraction. The sheer height and magnitude of the ride always rattled my nerves. Every time we were suspended in air, the wind brushed against the side of the cages, causing them to rock back and forth as my heart sank. "Oh no, we're tipping over. We're gonna die!" I cried in hysteria.

The merry-go-round, on the other hand, was a delight for the whole family. It was a beautiful and magnificent ride. It was adorned with hand-carved and hand-painted horses and brilliant lights cascading from the walls. Our faces were drawn with smiles with every revolution of the ride. The pulsing and wonderful carousel music added to the joyous experience. One ride in particular that I was deathly afraid of was the hammer. It was a rather simple ride with two ends that catapulted its riders into the air going in circles. My brother and I rode it together. With every turn, I screamed as far as the ear could hear. My brother laughed. I shouted at my parents as they stood on the sidelines watching. With tears in my eyes, I yelled at them, "Take me of! Take me off! Get me off this thing! Argh!"

My loving and highly concerned parents responded to my pain and agony in the face of certain death by laughing hysterically. Once I exited the ride, my parents consoled me by treating me to snacks— cotton candy, popcorn, hotdogs, candy apples, corn on the cob, etc.

Our family also played all the carnival games. We won several prizes such as teddy bears, goldfish, and other cool items. It was a magical time for our family. Unfortunately, Mountain Park no longer exists today. Now, only an empty lot stands in place of this once thriving mecca of euphoria.

Another great amusement park that our family spent many joyous moments together at was Riverside Park in Agawam, Massachusetts. Riverside was much bigger than Mountain Park and had much better attractions and rides. People came from far and wide. The parking lot was always full of cars and buses. The biggest draw for Riverside Park though was their extensive amount of death-defying roller coasters. Upon entering, you could ride a monorail that traveled from one end of the park to the other. It was sort of like a subway train. They also had a sky lift, which lifted the rider into the clear blue sky. From that point of view, you could witness the park in all its majestic glory. The aromas that permeated from the park's restaurants were appetite enhancing. We took several short breaks during the day and enjoyed the fine cuisine that the park offered. After a good meal, we warmed up with all the smaller and less-threatening rides.

After some well-deserved rest, it was time to set off for the ride of all rides: the Black Widow. It was a behemoth of a ride. It catapulted riders forward at a spine-tingling speed and then dropped them sharply as it made a gut-wrenching loop to the top of the ride. You were left catching your breath for a few seconds, then were sent flying backward the same way. Most frightened riders got off at the end of the ride with pale blank looks on their faces. Many riders threw up on the stairwells on their way down from the ride as well. One too many beers, I guess. Our family stayed in the park until closing. It was great to see all the rides and attractions light up with colorful blinking lights underneath the night sky.

On our way home, we made a stop at the local McDonalds. I always ate two small cheeseburgers with a small fry and a strawberry shake. I always took out the pickles and gave them to my brother. He always had two Big Macs with fries and a large Coke. Mom and Dad always consumed their usual burgers with fries as well. Great times with my family. Riverside Park is now Six Flags Park. Yup.

18. Olympic Games, 1976

Nadia Comăneci, Sugar Ray Leonard, Bruce Jenner, Edwin Moses, Leon Spinks, Michael Spinks, Howard Davis Jr., and many others were shining stars at the Montreal Games. Nadia Comăneci scored the first ten in history on the high bar in gymnastics, securing the gold for Romania. Sugar Ray Leonard won the gold medal in boxing for the USA, joining the likes of Muhammad Ali and George Foreman. Sugar Ray, like Ali, was also trained by the late great Angelo Dundee. Bruce Jenner won gold in the decathlon. The year 1976 was a great year for American athletes, and they were showcased on boxes of Wheaties cereal. Millions of Americans woke up to breakfast with the faces of champions staring back at them. I must say, it was good way to start the day. As a child, I was extremely motivated by the Olympians performances. I always imagined myself standing atop of the podium, winning a gold medal for team USA. Every four years after, I sat in front of the television every time the games came on. It was an exhilarating experience that still continued with me to this day. Yup.

19. Detectives, Busted, 1976

My first few years as a kid were happy and joyous. Amusement parks, drive-in movies, beaches, zoos, parks, circus, fishing, picnics, church on Sundays, apple picking in the orchards, and a wide array of other activities were an integral part of my childhood. I always watched the *Leave It to Beaver* TV show. I saw myself like Beaver Cleaver. I viewed my older brother like Wally Cleaver. The Cleavers lived the perfect life. They were the perfect TV family with a beautiful house, car, dog, and a white picket fence. Every time there was a problem on the show, the Cleavers resolved it with morals and family values. Beaver's parents were always very supportive, understanding, and indispensable. Unlike the TV show, our real family life was quite another story.

As I got older and the years passed by, I became more aware of my family surroundings. My dad was a tall, hulking man and

25

an ominous figure. Dad was over six feet tall. He was loving yet very stern, affectionate, but at times withdrawn. Mom was lovingly warm and caring but very harshly demanding at times. I recalled it was 1976, and my dad and his friend Skip were in the Army. One night, while still wearing Army fatigues, they both came home with a cache of weapons. They had several machine guns and pistols. My dad stored the firearms underneath one of the living room couches. He sewed the bottom of the couch to keep the guns from dislodging and falling on the floor. He gave Edward and I a cold steely look and strictly warned and forbade us from playing on the sofa. We understood. Always excited and a bundle of energy, we both played and bounced around the other couches but kept our distance from the off-limits area.

One time, at about 2:00 a.m., I was awoken by loud sounds and shuffling in the living room. I was six years old at the time. I used to wet my bed frequently. My nerves were jittery. All sorts of stuffed animals adorned my bed. The Pink Panther, Winnie-the-Pooh, Piglet, Tigger, and a vast array of teddy bears kept me safe at night, or at least I thought. They were my devoted protectors or guardian angels so to speak. I felt if any monsters came out from underneath my bed or closet, they were dealt with swiftly. I was intensely afraid of the dark. I guess it was due to all the horror movies I had seen with my family at the drive-in theater. As I made my way to the living room with the Pink Panther in one hand and Winnie-the-Pooh in the other, I noticed light emanating from the living room and heard several voices.

As I continued down the long hallway and turned into the living room, bright lights suddenly shined upon my young unsuspecting face and temporarily blinded me. I covered my eyes as best I could using my stuffed animals as a shield. Once my vision had cleared up, I tried making out what was happening. My eyes opened wider than saucer plates in shock when I saw the man I looked up to—my protector, my provider, my loving dad—handcuffed with his hands behind his back to a chair. Mom was in tears and also handcuffed. A large amount of money was strewn all over the living room floor. My dad's arsenal of weapons was on display for all to see. I urinated my pajamas right then and there. It was too much for me to handle. The scene was right out of a movie.

Detectives were everywhere, all dressed up in three-piece suits with ties. I was very intrigued by their holstered guns. I never saw a detective before. Well, only in TV shows like *Starsky & Hutch*, *The Streets of San Francisco*, *Baretta*, *S.W.A.T.*, *The Rookies*, etc. I was totally amazed by cops on television. I used to always pretend being one. *What about Mom and Dad? Why are the detectives doing this to them?* I thought. Seeing me worried, the officers quickly tried calming me down. They laughed and joked with me, helping to alleviate my fears. Perhaps the law enforcement officers had children of their own and understood the frailties of such a young child witnessing such an event. Moments later, my aunt who lived upstairs came down for Edward and me. We spent the night upstairs.

The next day, Mom was released, innocent of any wrongdoing. My dad was arrested for drug trafficking and weapon possession. We often went to see him in prison. It became the routine for the next few years. Seeing Dad in orange prison garbs was very odd for me, but I knew he was being punished rightly so for his actions. I came to the stark realization at a very tender age that this wasn't the path I wanted to follow. Yup!

20. Apple Picking, 1977

Living in Springfield, Massachusetts, as a child was very refreshing. The lifestyle was rather slow but very family oriented. There were many parks, fields, lakes, and rivers in the area. Outdoor activities in natural surroundings were a major component of people's daily lives in Springfield. Our family spent many weekends fishing or having picnics in the park. Visiting the park zoo was also very enjoyable. The monkeys in the exhibits were very naughty and threw their dung or urine at the visitors. I must admit it was very funny. I remembered one day a monkey threw his pee at my dad. Hilarious! Dad wasn't too happy.

Apple picking at the orchards in the springtime was also a very pleasant experience. Occasionally, our family loaded the car and took long rides into the countryside on Sunday afternoons. We visited a family friend named Lucy. Our family lovingly referred to her as Lucy la Loca, translated "crazy Lucy." She studied at Amherst University in Massachusetts. She had two young daughters named Blanca and Sashi. Lucy was very cool, and I enjoyed spending time at her place with my family. She reminded me of the rock and roll singer Janice Joplin. Lucy was a very eccentric lady. She collected many exotic weapons and hung them on her wall, all sorts of swords and bow and arrows. She was also an animal lover. She had dogs, turtles, birds, and a large snake.

Eventually, she moved with her kids to Brooklyn. She lived in a rough part of Brooklyn. We visited her a few times but eventually lost contact with her. Throughout the years, I've always wondered what ever happened to her and her very nice daughters. Yup!

21. Vandalism, 1977

I've always respected police as the gatekeepers of law and order. By the time I was seven years old, my parents had several run-ins with the law. My relationship with cops began soon thereafter. One summer afternoon, my cousin Raymond, Edward, and I played across the street from the building we lived in. We messed around in the backyard of an elementary school. We carried on like juvenile delinquents. We made a loud ruckus by throwing garbage and debris around the schoolyard without a care in the world. All of us grew up on the rough side of the tracks. Perhaps we acted out and vented the hostility we felt in our own personal life. We all pounded on the back door of the school. We threw rocks at the windows, breaking a few in the process. An old abandoned tricycle was nearby, so we decided to slam it against the door for good measure as well. We were like the Little Rascals from hell.

Suddenly, a car came screeching down the street, like a scene from a 1970s TV cop show. It was the fuzz. The police. "Oh my God!" I said in a panic. Actually, all of us panicked. Tears started rolling down my cheek. *I'm going to jail forever!* I thought. They quickly rolled up on us and jumped out of the cruiser. Two large cops, one

White and Black cop. They had big guns and handcuffs. I was so scared. Absolutely terrified! "Get on the wall and put your hands up!" both officers shouted drawing their guns. All of us were lined up against the schoolyard wall with our feet spread apart. We got frisked and the whole nine yards, and they even read us our rights. My brother and cousin were spooked.

The officers chuckled under their breath. One officer looked over at the other and said, "I think we should cut them a break." The Black officer agreed. The first officer turned to us and said, "We're going to turn our backs and count to ten, you'd better be gone when we're done!." That was our cue to split. Both of them turned and started counting out loud, "One, two, three…" We took off like frightened rats. The three of us raced down the street, running as fast as humanly possible. We zipped across the street and ran through the driveway of our building. We flew up the stairs of the back porch that led to our apartments. My brother and I lived on the third floor. We tried catching our breath as we peeked through the curtains to see if the officers were gone. Yup!

22. Elvis's Death, 1977

I grew up listening to Elvis's music throughout the 1970s. My dad used to watch all his films on TV. They usually played on Sundays during the Elvis marathon—*Blue Hawaii, Viva Las Vegas, King Creole, Jailhouse Rock, G.I. Blues, Roustabout, The Trouble with Girls*, etc. The music was very cool. My two favorite songs were "Jailhouse Rock" and "Hound Dog." He shook and strutted his stuff for the ladies' delight. The young Elvis in the '60s was slim and trim, but the 1970s version was overweight. Regardless, he could still fire up the crowd. His very colorful and dazzling outfits were outlandish and larger than life. When the music came on, it was a madhouse of energy. Sadly, it was reported that Elvis had passed away on August 16, 1977. It was all over the news, and I was deeply saddened by his demise. A legend was gone, but his music lives on forever. Yup!

23. Dad's Friend Skip, 1977

My dad had a cool white friend named Skip. He looked like Shaggy from the *Scooby-Doo* cartoon. They were buddies who both served in the US military. They did everything together. They were inseparable. Skip lived across town from us. Our family visited him several times a year. Skip was an avid collector of exotic pets. He had snakes, mice, lizards, birds, etc. He kept a gigantic python in a large cage. It always looked ready to eat something. Hopefully, that something wasn't me. I always kept my distance from the cage. I could see it following my movements with its cold, steely beady eyes. Left to right, right to left, it surely had me on its radar. Its body pulsed as its tongue slithered in and out in search of a morsel. I thought, *Could I be on its menu?* The top of the cage was slightly cracked open, and in went a small white mouse. The cute little rodent made its way around the far edges of the cage when, to its surprise, it momentarily came face to face with its executioner. The mouse stood frozen in time as its heart slowed down so as not to arouse its—*chomp*! Sigh! The little mouse was now only a memory and a figment of my imagination.

Skip also had a very large dog, a Great Dane. His name was Bolo, just like the character in Bruce Lee's *Enter the Dragon*. One day, he dropped by our house in his replica Scooby-Doo van. Edward and I were playing in the backyard. Suddenly, a gargantuan beast exited from the back of his vehicle. We panicked as both our eyes met its "Time for din din eyes". The horse-sized monstrosity sized us up like two Big Macs and must've thought that we were its dinner.

He suddenly chased us around the yard for what seemed like an eternity. We ran in circles, screaming like two newborn babies, trying our best not to be trampled by the behemoth. We were scared out of our wits! Skip yelled out, "Bolo, Bolo, Bolo!" Finally, the beast disengaged and returned to his owner in the nick of time. I was ready to pee my pants! Yup!

24. Grandma's Burial in Puerto Rico, 1977

Grandma relocated from the South Bronx to Springfield, Massachusetts. It was great being able to see her all the time. Mom always picked her up at her apartment on Waverly Street. It was an apartment that she shared with my uncle Pepin (Jose). Our family always went to church with Grandma and then out to dinner soon afterward. Some nights, when Grandma visited our home, the rest of our family gathered together, including my aunts Juanita and Julia with all their kids and my uncle Pepin as well. One Easter night, the whole family watched *The Ten Commandments* starring Charlton Heston on TV.

Grandma made us food and served us coffee every time we visited her apartment. She had beautiful long white flowing hair, which actually looked silver, that stretched to her lower back. She hugged me and read to me from her Old Testament Bible. "Be a good boy and always pray every night before going to bed," she constantly and lovingly reminded me. The night before Grandma died, she had a vision, which she revealed to my uncle Pepin the next morning over breakfast. She said, "Last night while praying, I suddenly felt a cold presence in the room. I decided to take a closer look, and I was surprised to see Mom's spirit gesturing with her hand for me to follow her." My grandmother passed away the very next night, on April 13, 1977. I was very close to my grandmother. She was my guardian angel. She was a very religious and spiritual woman. I was traumatized. Totally heartbroken. I couldn't fathom that my beloved grandma was gone. I was only six years old and too young to lose my grandmother.

On April 15, our family—which included several aunts, uncles, Mom, and me—boarded an Eastern Airlines flight at John F. Kennedy Airport in New York en route to Puerto Rico. My young eyes witnessed when they loaded my grandmother's coffin onto the plane. I now believed that Grandma was an angel of God and would protect me everywhere I went. I was fascinated with the large jumbo jets. I shouted, "Mommy, Mommy, look, look! as the plane pulled out of the tarmac. Mom was terrified of flying. I, on the other hand, was having a ball, not aware of the ever-present danger. I kept looking out of the small windows of the airplane as we took off down the runway. The plane picked up speed. My family prayed. The plane lifted off the runway and took flight as everyone gasped. We were in flight for three hours. I was my usual hyperactive self. I bounced off the seats and ran to the toilet as much as possible. My mother took a nap. Poor Mom. She was totally exhausted from the whole event.

A few minutes later, the stewardess brought out snacks and refreshments. Yummy! Then a movie screen came down in front of the plane. It was then and there that I got my first glimpse of *Rocky*. I was captivated. The story drew me in. The training sequence totally blew my mind. My mouth dropped. "Rocky, Rocky, Rocky!" I yelled at the screen while pumping my fist into the air. I was filled with excitement. At the end of the film, Rocky was left battered and bruised. I felt his pain more than ever. Perhaps it was due to my own tragic loss. I somehow understood his agony and torment. I fell in love with the movie.

We finally arrived at our destination. Everyone clapped and cheered as we landed. Thank God. As we departed the plane, I felt the warm ocean breeze against me. I heard the palm trees crackling in the wind. The smell in the air was so fresh and tropical. The beautiful island of Puerto Rico. My uncle picked us up at the airport. We lovingly referred to him as Tio Cholo. He was one of my mother's older brothers. I was very nervous and hyper. I kept jumping on my seat and peering out the window at the local landscape. Eventually, we reached our destination. We arrived in Carolina, Puerto Rico.

I was shocked with what I saw next. It was something I'd never seen before. Lizards, lizards, and more lizards. They were everywhere—on the ground, walls, fences, trees, rooftops, automobiles, and every place you can imagine. They all looked like miniature versions of Godzilla and totally creeped me out. For the first few days, I was very tentative and kept my distance. Mom said, "Don't be afraid. They won't hurt you." So with Mom's encouraging words, I mustered up the courage to approach the small dinosaur-looking reptiles. I tried sneaking up on one lizard as he quickly bolted. I was startled and jumped back in astonishment. My uncle belted out a laugh in his loud, booming Barry White–like voice. The next day, I kept trying to muster up the courage to seize one of the elusive creatures. When I was at my wits end and felt like it was all but impossible, I finally hit paydirt and caught one of the critters. On another occasion, I grabbed one by the tail. The lizard quickly slithered from side to side, detaching its body from its tail, and ran off, leaving its dismembered limb wiggling in my grasp. My cousin remarked, "Don't grab them by the tail. They do that in self-defense." He then proceeded to hold one up by the tail. To my dismay, the same thing happened. My cousin was left with the tail bouncing in his hand. My cousin said, "That's how they escape from predators."

I started collecting lizards and placing them in milk containers. My mother wasn't too happy with my newfound hobby. Everywhere I traveled, I plundered as many lizards as I could fit into my container. I only focused on small unassuming lizards, staying away from the much larger and menacing iguanas. "Pick up the big ones, my son," Mom said lovingly. *Hell no!* I thought. They were huge and could probably bite my finger off. Regardless, I continued my campaign hunting the tiniest lizards I could find. The local kids let the lizards bite and hang off their earlobes like a pair of earrings. I learned to do likewise. My mother must've thought I was nuts.

One afternoon, Mom and my aunts decided to go shopping in San Juan. I brought a large container of lizards with me. Mom was so caught up in her shopping and chatting with my aunts that she never noticed the package I was carrying. Lo and behold, as all the woman were trying on clothing and yapping away, I decided to take a peep into my container that suddenly became eerily silent. *Hmm,* I wondered, as I peered into the darkness of the gallon-sized carton. Suddenly, with all their fury, the army of lizards rushed full throttle out of the container. It was a major exodus. Several landed on my chest, face, arms, and shoulders. I shrieked as I hoisted the reptile-infested container into the air. It landed on the floor with a loud, ear-piercing thud! Like buffalos roaming the plains, the lizards took off in all directions at once. Unexpectedly, the women took notice of the debacle and began screaming reminiscent of bangies in the ghostly hours of the night. The women scattered like roaches, facing sure death from a can of Raid. They zigzagged between aisles, knocking one another over, disregarding their ladylike manners. They jumped onto chairs, shelves, and clothing racks, trying to escape the carnage before them. I did my best to gather as many escaped convicts as I could, but my mother knocked the container out of my hand and reprimanded me. End of story.

Puerto Rico was very hot and humid. Trees bearing fruit such as bananas, mangos, guayabas, coconuts, etc. grew everywhere. It was a tropical paradise. During the evenings, my cousin, a couple of local kids, and myself snuck into the neighbors' yards. We were some sneaky-ass kids. We snatched quenapas from high up in the trees. Quenapas are similar to green grapes except that they have large seeds inside and taste bittersweet. Plus, you need to crack the outer shells to reveal the fruit inside. Yummy! All of us kids were great at climbing and scaling trees.

Some mornings, my cousin Junito and I played outside. My cousin owned a go-kart. We raced our go-kart against other kids. Most go-karts were handmade, usually made with the wheels and bottom frames of a shopping cart. A wooden plank was placed on top of the frame and tied to the end of a string to shift and turn it. We all gathered on top of a hill and thrusted ourselves toward the bottom at top speed. The races were heated. Down the hill all day long. Wee! It felt like I was racing in the Daytona 500.

I made friends with some local cats—well, actually kittens. They were a small litter of five to six kittens. They were born underneath the porch of my aunt Candita's home. I played with them every day. They were adorable and cuddly like teddy bears. I carried and embraced them as much as possible. They were my babies, or so I thought. Mama cat wanted to scratch my eyes out. She attacked and scratched me several times in defense of her young. I loved the kittens, and I would never put them in harm's way, but nevertheless, she wasn't having any of it.

With every opportunity, she made her move and turned me into her scratching post. I had marks all over my face and body. She constantly hissed at me and chased me away. Regardless, every chance I had, I snuck the kittens away. My mom kept scolding me and yelling, "Put those dirty animals down!" but her words fell on deaf ears. There was another problem: the kittens were infested with fleas, lots and lots of fleas! I was so itchy. They were consuming and devouring my flesh. My body was a constellation of insect bites. My mother had enough. Together with my aunt Candita she placed your truly and all the kittens into a large bucket.It was overflowing with hot water and soap and suds. Scrub a dub, dub into the tub. Goodbye kittens.

Our family held my grandmother's wake in my uncle Mario's home. It was a mad house. My aunts and uncles were all present. They numbered about twenty in all. Dozens of my cousins were also present to show their respects. All the children, including myself, played outside. Some of my aunts made heaping pots of food and coffee. I stuffed my face and drank about a gallon of coffee with multiple spoons of sugar in each cup. I was wired. A sugar rush to the maximum. The children were buzzing around like bees on a nest. We played through the wee hours of the night till our bones ached, totally impervious to the suffering our parents were subjected to. We were too young and naive.

The funeral procession the next morning was enormous. There were cars for blocks and blocks. So many beautiful reefs and flowers were displayed on top of the vehicles. We drove slowly for a few miles underneath the hot, melting sun until we finally arrived at the cemetery. Everyone was so well dressed. It sort of reminded me of my parents' wedding day, but this was a sad occasion. Everyone was in tears as the holy man read from the Bible, "From ashes to ashes and dust to dust." My grandma was then lowered into the grave as my family shrieked with cries from deep within their souls, which pierced and penetrated the calm air of the tropic day. I lowered my head and truly understood at this defining moment that Grandma was gone forever. I love you, Abuelita. Bially. Yup.

25. Yankees, 1977

Being from the Bronx, I was naturally inclined to be a Yankees fan. The Yankees are undoubtedly the greatest baseball team in history. I felt much pride being born in the Boogie Down Bronx. I wore my Yankee gear all the time. I often argued with other kids about which team was the best, especially against Red Sox fans. I couldn't stand the Red Sox fans. They were arrogant and conceited, or so I thought. I always spoke of the greats, greats like Babe Ruth and Joe DiMaggio, but the 1970s belonged to Reggie Jackson.

Mr. October ripped three home runs during the sixth game of the World Series against the Los Angeles Dodgers on October 18, 1977. Jackson hit three home runs in a row off of three consecutive pitches from three different pitchers. This amazing feat helped the Yankees win the game and the championship. Thurman Munson was also vital as a pitcher to the franchise. Unfortunately, he died in an airplane crash soon after.

I wanted to follow in the footsteps of the all-time greats. I watched *The Bad News Bears* movie at the local drive-in theater. I loved everything about the film. Later on, I tried out for a local little league team, the Van Horn Yankees. Luckily, I barely made the team. I was selected to play first base. In my first game, I caught a line drive for an out. My first time at bat, I hit a short drive toward the short stop, and I ran and slid into first base. My coach told me, "You don't slide into first." I was out. My uniform was dirty and muddy, but I felt cool about the whole experience. Bruce Lee soon came into my life, and that put an end to my baseball career. Yup.

26. Stray Dogs, 1977

There was a time when stray dogs roamed the neighborhood streets, sometimes alone or in packs. I always felt sorry for them. Most of them were hungry and homeless. I loved dogs. Not unlike many other kids, I wanted to be a veterinarian when I grew up. My intention was to rescue and save every poor animal I found on the street and provide a loving habitat for them. Well, every time I found a stray dog, I brought it home with me. I took a rope and tied it around the dog's neck. The dog undoubtedly was not a willing participant in the matter. It tried fighting its way out of the noose, but I was undeterred and wasn't going to be denied. I wholeheart-edly wanted this new addition to the family. So I dragged the poor, wretched animal all the way home. All for the sake of love. I only pulled this stunt with the smaller dogs, mind you. I didn't have the nerve to attempt this with the much larger and aggressive-natured canines. No siree Bob.

My parents weren't very thrilled with my new hobby—the local dog collector. My parents were very vocal and expressive about my new found endeavor, especially mom. "No me traiga perros sato a esta casa!" Mom yelled out numerous times, which meant "Don't bring any stray dogs home!" But did I listen? Nope! Every chance I got, I brought home some mangy stray. One in particular was a very adorable beagle. I really loved this pooch. He had long floppy ears and a cute button nose. The dog was absolutely charming. I spent all my time walking, feeding, and cuddling my beloved new pet.

One afternoon, after returning home from a long day at school, I noticed that my pooch had disappeared without a trace. "Oh no, where could he be?" I shuddered. Paranoia took over. I panicked and became utterly desperate in my futile attempt to find my hound. I looked all over the house—the backyard, the porch, the bushes, and the garage. Finally, I approached my parents in a last-ditch effort to locate my missing friend. "Did you see my dog?" I curiously asked my parents. They had a blank look on their faces, then came up with some silly story about how my dog ran away. I responded, "All the doors were locked!" My parents quickly snapped back, "He jumped out of the window." I was like, "Really, how could this be?" We lived on the second floor. It was just too high for the dog to leap down from. There was also an iron fence with sharp spikes at the bottom of the window. The dog would've been impaled. *Impossible!* I thought. However, my parents stuck to their story. But then I wondered, *If Rin Tin Tin and the bionic dog could jump it, then perhaps my dog could jump it too.*

I didn't want to accept that my pooch was gone. So I embarked on a mission to find him. I had some of the local neighborhood kids help me on my crusade. Finally, I was rewarded for all my hard work. I saw him in the distance. I shouted, "There he is!" I was ready with my rope. Once again, the beagle was in my possession. I quickly scurried him home. I was ecstatic and overjoyed. My parents had a smirk on their faces. *Why didn't they celebrate in my new found happiness?* I wondered. Oh well, I had my beloved pet back at least for the moment. This was short-lived however. The very next day, the dark clouds came rolling back in. Once again, I returned from school only to notice that my cuddly buddy was missing in action. As I walked in the door, everything was quiet, and I heard no barking. Where was my welcome home reception? Where were the paw prints all over my clothes? No wagging tails, panting, or sloppy smooches. Nothing.

My parents gave me the same old, tired story. They fed me a pack of lies. I became very suspicious and irate. I decided to further investigate the situation. So I put on my personal thinking cap. I was now an official private investigator/detective, just like the Baretta character on TV. I began my investigation by heading downstairs to the front entrance of the building. I surveyed the area. I looked up at my apartment. The windows were all closed. Like I said before, the fall was too high for my dog. My Beagle was tiny and had stout legs, and besides, that iron fence was impenetrable. My dog would've surely died from the impact.

I spent the next few weeks searching for my best friend. I canvassed the neighborhood day in and day out. I finally came to the conclusion that my Beagle was never coming back. My heart was broken. Sigh. A few days later, my brother confessed to me that my parents had driven my dog far away and got rid of him. I felt so betrayed. My poor little beagle. Oh, how I miss you!

Later on, I ran into another dog on the street. I scooped him up and named him Whitey. The reason being, because he was white. Most kids gave their dogs rather simple and unsophisticated names back then. If he was black, then you called him Blacky. That was it, simple and to the point. Anyway, I found this dirty, dingy, scruffy, and very smelly dog. He was perfect. Yes, Whitey! He had a wee-wee. You see, my parents didn't want female dogs in the house whatsoever. Male dogs were okay. So I always had to make sure the dog had a wee-wee.

He was a terrier mix. A mongrel. A mutt. His fur was lumpy and tangled, and his nails were unkempt, but all those things didn't mean squat to me. He was mine, and my new pooch was divine. So here I was, nine years old, chilling with my little furry friend, and happier than ever. I walked my dog up and down the block for all the envious kids to look at. My majestic king of a dog, the great Whitey! I crossed the street with my dog attached by a rope to my wrist. My parents were not going to buy a dog chain for some four-legged flea-bag I found on the street. So I made use of whatever was handy.

There was an older gentleman who lived across the street who owned two big dogs—real big dogs, a Great Dane and a Doberman pinscher. I lovingly nicknamed them King Kong and Godzilla. All of a sudden, the backyard screen door burst open, and his killer dogs from hell ran outside as they were unleashed on their carnivorous search for prey. They caught a whiff of my dog on their radar, and the chase commenced. My dog, being street smart as he was, quickly eluded their advance. He broke loose from my grip and went off running as fast his stubby little legs could carry him. I heard the galloping sounds of these monsters' paws as they smashed against the pavement. Kathump! Kathump! *Holy shit! Where do I hide? "Where do I run to?* I thought in my panicked state. I scaled the side of the building as Whitey took off like Scooby-Doo after seeing a ghost. His buddies were in hot pursuit. I cried loudly, "Run, Whitey, run!" Whitey made his way around the building and whizzed past me whimpering out loud. The monsters whizzed past me two seconds after that. The dogs ran one circle, two circles, and then three circles around the building. Whitey was panting, and his tongue was hanging out from the exhaustive chase. My poor, helpless mutt. I heard a whistle, a loud whistle. The man called off his massive machines of destruction. Whitey was temporarily safe. I scrambled off the wall and grabbed Whitey by his rope. I quickly ran home in tears with my pooch by my side. Another interesting day in the life of a child. Yup.

27. Family Gatherings, 1977

One of my favorite times as a kid was on the weekends. Whether it was getting up very early on Saturday mornings to watch cartoons or going to the beach, fishing, movies, dinner or some other family gathering on Sunday afternoons. Some weekends, my cousins would visit. It was party time! Mom started cooking early in the afternoon. Edward and I ran errands to the store to pick up any ingredients Mom needed for cooking.

The heavenly aroma permeated from the oven. A feast. She made pernil (roasted ham), arroz con gandules (yellow rice with peas), and a delectable salad. The scent of roasted ham adorned with pineapples, steaming rice, and freshly brewed coffee was tantalizing. At our house, we only drank Bustelo coffee, Puerto Rican coffee. It was very strong and potent. Exactly the way we liked it. My brother and I tossed the salad. Dad helped out with the cooking duties, well as much as he possibly could. It was a nice family moment.

A few moments later, a carload of people drove up and parked in front of the house. They were packed into the car like a bunch of circus clowns in a small vehicle. Yeah! I was ecstatic. We greeted everyone as they came in. My uncle Flaco, his wife Maritza, and my cousins Nukie, Macho, Charisse, and Baby. Salsa music was blaring from our record player. Héctor Lavoe, El Gran Combo, Ismael Rivera, Celia Cruz, Willie Colón, Rubén Blades, Cheo Feliciano, and countless others. I loved those albums.

Mom told us kids to go outside and play. It was a good way to get the kids out of the adults' hair for a while. The adults gathered in the living room to chat. Mom went into the kitchen and brought out hot coffee and snacks. Dad and my uncle played several games of chess. Dad loved chess and taught me how to play when I was knee-high. Mom once again shouted, "Go outside!" This time with a much stronger tone and a stern look on her face. We clearly got the message this time. We zigzagged our way through the house and busted out the front door like a pack of wild chimpanzees escaping from the zoo.

We gathered outside with other kids from the neighborhood. We played tag, cops and robbers, cowboys and Indians, red rover, freeze tag, red light–green light, mother may I, city chase, manhunt, hide-and-seek, etc. A few hours passed, and it started getting dark. The scent of the food caught our hungry bellies. Mom yelled, "Come inside for dinner!" We all washed up and sat down at the dinner table. We devoured all our food void of table manners of any sort. After dinner, the kids went to the attic and played with toys, board games, or acted silly dilly.

Later that evening, our parents got dressed, ready to hit the town for a night of disco dancing. This was what all of us kids were waiting for. Yes! My brother was the designated babysitter. He was the oldest and most responsible. He'd make sure that we were all well behaved. Yeah right. Okay. I didn't think so. He was a conspirator for our dirty deeds. Ha ha! Our parents left the house dressed in polyester suits, satin dresses, platform shoes, and high-heeled pumps. They had on their best threads. They all looked like they were auditioning for *Saturday Night Fever*. As soon as they left and the coast was clear, the balloons and party hats came out. Hurray!

The first thing we did was raid the refrigerator. We hastily snatched the Doritos, Cheese Doodles, Twinkies, Hottess cupcakes, Maltas, Coca-Cola, ice cream, and anything else we could possibly plunder from the fridge. Yummy, yummy! We all sat by the television set with our snacks in hand, watching scary movies. We watched classic horror shows such as *Chiller* and *Fright Night*. We had the best time of our lives. We played jokes on one another, ran all over the house, jumped on our beds, wrestled, played loud music, and told ghosts stories. My brother always tried spooking us by hiding or making strange, creepy sounds. It usually worked, and we trembled uncontrollably. We had a blast. We all finally crashed and fell asleep.

Our parents returned home at the crack of dawn. They didn't make a sound. We woke up and had breakfast cereal with milk—Frosted Flakes, Apple Jacks, Lucky Charms, Fruity Pebbles, Corn Pops, Franken Berry, Boo Berry, Count Chocula, Fruit Loops, etc. All us kids sat down in front of the TV set while watching cartoons with happy faces and a big bowl of cereal in our laps. Hours later, our parents were still knocked out with a hangover. Good times! Yup.

28. El Cuco, Night Monsters, 1977

Children from all different cultures have grown up with spooky stories of creatures that go roaming in the night—monsters, ghosts, spirits, the supernatural, and other strange and macabre occurrences that take place after hours. For most Puerto Rican kids are most grisly and dreaded fear was "El Cuco". A hideous diabolical monster that consumed and devoured all the flesh and souls of all naughty children who were unruly and blatantly disobeyed their parents or loved ones. It came at night while you were sleeping. It lurked under your bed, in the closet, behind the curtain, and within all dark spaces and crevices. The shadows were its domain. You couldn't escape the entity. Children had no idea what El Cuco exactly looked like, but it must've been disarranged and deformed, with long fangs and claws, hairy and scary, a monstrosity in every sense of the word. A beast.

The dark and ominous creature was summoned from the netherworld into our midst. Of course, this was all bullshit, but what did we know. Kids in the 1970s grew up watching horror movies, the likes of *Dracula, Frankenstein, The Mummy, The Wolfman, The Exorcist, The Omen,* etc. Horror was etched in our psyche. When parents pulled that El Cuco card, we responded in full with sheer panic and fear. We sat our asses down and listened and behaved from thereon, well at least till the next moment of misbehavior. "Ouiii! Ouiii!" was the growling voice emanating from the shadows. We were scared shitless!

My brother took full advantage of the situation. On the weekends, we stood up late at night watching *Chiller* or *Fright Night.* They showcased scary movies from the 1950s to the 1970s. Edward hid behind the couch while I was engaged watching the movies horrifying and intense scenes in utter shock. He then slowly snuck his hand up and around from behind the sofa and gently tapped me on the shoulder and said, "Oui!" I jumped up from my seat in a heartbeat, shivering and rattled in tears. Poor me, I was only about seven years old at the time. After spending some time calming me down, my demented brother with his devilish grin said, "Please get me some Doritos from the kitchen."

I sheepishly replied, "No, you're going to scare me!"

"No, I'm not. I promise, I swear to God!" he shot back.

"Okay," I responded. I believed him. What a sucker I was.

There was a very long hallway that led to the kitchen from the living room. The light switch for the kitchen was in the living room. The hallway was very dark. Pitch-black. I told my brother, "Turn on the kitchen light." He turned it on. As I made my way down the long corridor, I glanced over my shoulder, looked at Edward, and told him, "Remember, you promised."

"Yeah, yeah!" he shouted back.

I tiptoed my way to the refrigerator, looking all around the room in fear, thinking some creature was about to leap at me from the cupboards or shelves. My brother kept a close eye on me from the other room while standing next to the light switch in a rather sinister manner. I was in a precarious situation. *Could I trust Edward, or should I make a dash for the living room?* I thought. I decided to continue forward. I dug deep into the fridge and poured Edward and myself a plate of Doritos and two cups of soda as well. All was good.

It was time to head back to the comfy couch to watch the rest of the movie undeterred. Boom! The lights went out. "Ouiii!" said the bellowing voice. My loving and trusting confidante, my brother Edward, had failed me. Batman had let Robin down. How could this be. "Argh!" I yelled as far as my voice could reach. Everything, and I do mean everything, I held in my hands flew up in the air. Splash, thud, and crash were the loud sounds the objects made when they hit the floor. I sped through the long, narrow hallway and was back in the living room in a flash. "You liar, you liar!" I cried. Edward couldn't contain himself with his evil laughter. My crazy-ass brother! Yup! Ha ha.

29. Aunt Juanita, 1977

My aunt Jenny and her three children used to live in a roughneck part of town in Springfield, Massachusetts. They lived on Waverly Street, on the third floor of an old tenement. My uncle Pepin lived on the first floor. He shared an apartment with my grandmother who recently moved from the Bronx. We spent many hours visiting my aunt and grandmother. My aunt and Mom always sat down in the kitchen while they sipped a cup of coffee, played cards, and chatted for hours.

The kids, on the other hand, always went outside to play. We always made a stop at the local grocery store to get some ice cream sandwiches. They cost was only a mere five cents each. Delightful. "Yummy!" we all said to one another in sheer delight as the ice cream melted and dripped from our hands. We ran around the neighborhood, exploring all that could be explored. We played street games with the other kids from the area. We also bought tons of bubblegum, competing to see who could blow the biggest bubbles. Bazooka Joe was the favorite gum for most kids at the time. It had a miniature comic inside the wrapping. We also spent quality time at the local library reading up on our favorite stories. *Curious George* and *A Cat in the Hat* were two of my favorite books. I loved to read.

Every time the carnival was in town, we had tons of fun riding *las machinas*, which translated in Spanish meant "amusement rides." The traveling gypsies usually set up rides in abandoned parking lots. We gathered our bit of change so that we could play the carnival games. At dusk, the rides lit up with bright and vivid colorful lights and the smell of fresh popcorn and cotton candy flowing through the air. Our parents eventually joined us and bought us a few tickets so we could get on some of the rides. It was great being a kid in the 1970s. On early Saturday mornings, all the kids sat in front of the television to watch cartoons. *Scooby-Doo* was my cousin Michelle's favorite. Michelle was my older cousin. She always had a sense of humor and took care of her younger siblings. She always had coloring books, dot-to-dot books, and tons of crayons. She was very creative. She was great at tracing and coloring. I learned how to trace by mimicking her movements. Her siblings Debbie and Raymond, a.k.a. Junior, did likewise. My brother Edward had some skills and drew as well.

One evening, my older cousin Maria Judy babysat the kids. My brother and I were back home. My cousin Raymond was playing with matches. The rundown apartment was infested with roaches. It seemed that he wanted to enact his revenge on the critters. His motive was to torture them one by one by igniting them all on fire, which he did, but he also accidently burned his own mattress in the process as well. The apartment was quickly engulfed in flames. My older cousin Maria Judy ran to the kitchen and hastily filled pots and pans with water to fight the fire with. She tried valiantly to subdue the fire, but it was to no avail. Thank goodness everyone was able to escape safely. Yup.

30. Edward Fight, 1977

Dad always taught Edward and me not to be chumps. He was very rough around the edges, a very old-school Puerto Rican. My brother and I grew up watching cartoons and playing with toys and board games. We were rather normal kids, so to speak. To the contrary, Dad lived a very tough childhood on the island. His basic overall philosophy was not to take any crap from anyone.

Edward and I spent most of our summer days playing outside with other kids in the neighborhood. In the 1970s, children learned how to get along with one another through close interaction. Social skills were developed on the streets. Bullies were common. Edward was very strong but rather introverted. One bully took notice. He kept chastising and insulting my brother every day. "You faggot!" he constantly shouted at him. My brother was tired of being humiliated and embarrassed and finally opened up and told Dad. Dad was very angry. He took Edward to the boy's house. He spoke with the bully's father. They both agreed that Edward and the bully should duke it out to resolve the issue.

So they let the boys fight it out right on the corner of the block. They squared off. My dad said, "My son is not a faggot! Kick his ass, son!" I, of course, wholeheartedly rooted for my brother. "Yeah, yeah, get 'em, Edward!" I shouted ecstatically from the sidelines. Edward put it on him and whupped him good. The boy, in a moment of despair, bit down on my poor brother's finger. Edward howled and cried in pain as the fight was brought to an end. The boy left the affair with bruises on his face and a few lumps on his noggin. My dad tended to my brother's wound as we made our way home. End of problem. Yup!

31. Driving, Highways, 1978

Road trips were a big deal for my family growing up. Dad always drove on the long-distance trips. On rare occasions, Mom drove for a few miles, cutting Dad a break. Our family often traveled from Massachusetts to New York and New Jersey to visit friends and relatives. Dad always sped down the freeway with the radio blaring. Great music bounced off the airwaves in them days. I really loved the song "Oh, What a Night." It was a great tune by Frankie Valli. When it came on, I sung all the lyrics word-for-word. "Staying Alive" and "Night Fever" by the Bee Gees were also great. "Don't Go Breaking My Heart" sung by Captain & Tennille was awesome as well. Another song that really moved me was a hit "Miracles" by Jefferson Starship. It had such beautiful harmonies and overtones. The great crooner Barry Manilow's classic song "It Could Be Magic" also stirred my soul. The lovely piano introduction was absolutely mesmerizing. Peter Brown's "Dance with Me" was fantastic too and had incredible vocals.

I loved flying down the freeway with the windows open. I always stuck my hand out the window, waving it through the thrashing wind. Edward did the same. We both made funny voices by sticking our faces out the window. Mom yelled out from the passenger seat, "Stop that! That's dangerous!" My brother and I cracked jokes at each other and bounced around the back seat, wrestling and carrying on. We were very hyperactive kids. I guess it was too much sugar. We'd make pit stops at the Howard Johnsons that were off the side of the I-95 highway. We'd get some food, use the restrooms, and then jump back into the car to continue on our long, arduous journey.

Other times, when no restrooms were available, we had to go commando. Dad stopped the car on the side of the road and yelled, "Everybody out! Hurry up!" The family jumped out of the car and ran into the woods and relieved themselves. We then quickly returned to the car and zoomed off. I loved them days! Sometimes, Edward and I waved at the 18-wheeler tractor trailers as they drove by. To our delight, the truck drivers blew their horns. The sound was deafening. We loved it! There were several tolls in Connecticut en route to New York, about three or four. I always got excited when we reached the New York Thruway toll.

We always entered the Bronx through the Co-op City side. There was a city bus depot on the left side of the freeway. *So many buses*, I thought. I excitedly looked out for the elevated subway lines. Graffiti adorned the subway cars. We were now officially in the Bronx, my place of birth. It was time to celebrate. Our car had an eight-track stereo. Dad popped in a tape. Salsa music—the likes of Héctor Lavoe, Ismael Rivera, Willie Colón, Cheo Feliciano, etc. Party time. Yup!

32. Breaking Night with Annie, 1978

My cousin Annie arrived from Puerto Rico in 1977. My mom and dad picked her up at the airport. She was a few years older than Edward and me. The day she arrived, we spent the night glued to the TV, eating junk food, and playing board games. We played Monopoly for hours. I had so much energy and was considered hyperactive. I couldn't sleep a wink! It must have been all the sugary products I consumed back then. My cousin was very cheery and sweet. Annie told us quite a few stories about her life growing up in Puerto Rico, mostly in Spanish, of course. My brother and I listened intently. She also told us a few *chistes* (jokes). Juan Bobo was one of the most popular and charismatic Puerto Rican characters she joked of. Ghost stories were next. She definitely got my attention with her spooky tales of the supernatural occurrences on the island.

After spending several hours getting to know our cousin from the Caribbean, we noticed a ray of light shining between the curtain into the room from outside. "Wow, it's daytime!" I said out loud in disbelief. I opened the curtain to further view the splendor of the morning sunrise. It was the first time in my young years that I had broken night. I was totally amazed. We had a wonderful time with our cousin, but then, it was time to get some shut-eye. So we said our good nights—well, actually, our good mornings—and then headed off to the land of sweet dreams. Yup.

33. Riding a Bike, 1978

I learned to ride a bike the hard way: downhill with no brakes. My cousin Jesus, a.k.a. Chuito, had just arrived to Springfield, Massachusetts, from Puerto Rico. He was Annie's younger brother and was a few years older than me. He was very good with bikes—riding them, taking them apart, and then rebuilding them with makeshift parts. His brother Willie arrived to Springfield a few years later. On one sunny summer afternoon, he decided to teach a few of the neighborhood kids how to ride a bike. This included my other cousin Raymond, my brother, and myself. Chuito's methods of teaching bike riding were rather simple and to the point. You didn't have to be a genius to learn. You basically got on a bike that was facing a steep, long downhill, and he pushed you to the bottom. That was it. Nothing fancy. Nothing complicated. "Oh by the way, hold on to the handlebars tightly, and don't forget to turn at the bottom" were his only instructions.

My cousin Raymond was the first poor victim to go racing down into the bottomless pit. Chuito grabbed the rear side of Raymond's bike with him seated on top of it. Chuito propelled him downhill with a mighty thrust of his arms. Raymond went flying toward the bottom at top speed with a little help from Chuito and the pull of gravity. Raymond tried turning at the end of the slope but failed in his attempt and crashed with a mighty thud into a row of trees. It was my turn next. I was sure that I would be able to conquer this hill. It was my first time riding a bike without training wheels. Chuito hoisted me up onto the bike and said, "Just keep the handlebars straight and then turn when you reach the bottom."

"Sure, sure, I got it!" I responded rather impatiently.

Chuito said, "Ready, one, two, three, go," and off I went. I held on for dear life, making sure to keep the handlebars straight as I was instructed to. I didn't realize how quickly I'd reach the bottom. I smacked into a fence and flipped right over the top of it onto the other side. I got up and laughed and waved to them that I was all right. My brother and a few other kids tried as well but were met with limited success. It was a great experience and a whole lot of fun. Yup!

34. Bus Accident, 1978

Mom taught me how to walk to the school bus stop on my own in the fall of 1978. I used to wait for the yellow school bus every day at 7:30 a.m. After a few days, I started getting the hang of it. The bus monitor always made sure that everyone got on the bus safely. One morning, I wasn't paying close enough attention, and I miscalculated my steps as the bus pulled in to the stop. It ran over my foot. My foot started throbbing in pain just like episodes of *Bugs Bunny* where the victim gets hit on the head and the lumps reveal themselves. I howled out in agony and took off down the street like a frightened rabbit. The bus monitor chased after me like a fox. I ran all the way to my apartment building and scooted up to the fourth floor, where I lived. The monitor finally caught up with me as Mom opened the door. She was totally out of breath. She did her best to explain to mom what had just happened. My mom understood and quickly took me to the hospital. The doctors took X-rays of my foot. I was lucky enough to escape only with bruises. The next day, I was laid up in bed with a bandage on my foot and a free day off from school. Lucky me. Yup.

35. Firefighter, the Jerk, 1978

I've always respected firefighters for their life-saving efforts and heroics during an emergency. Hearing the sirens and watching the firetrucks race down the street to help victims was always exhilarating for me as a kid. I'd race up to the window and eagerly waved at them in astonishment as they whizzed by. Sometimes, to my surprise, they'd wave back at me. TV shows were full of firefighters and cops in the 1970s, great shows that depicted them in a positive light, and for the most part, they were always on the right side of law and order.

There was a gentleman who lived on our block. The gentleman seemed rather cool and chatted with most of the kids in the neighborhood. He was very friendly and well-liked by the local building residents. He worked as a local fireman. Occasionally, I'd see him come out of his apartment in firefighting attire, just like the characters I saw on television. One day, a bunch of kids, including myself, were playing in the neighborhood. We horsed around and played all types of street games. There was a sleek black car parked on the block. It was a beautiful Cutlass Supreme. Its windows were rolled down. A few of us kids were eating slices of cheese. We started playing around with our food and threw pieces at one another. One of my small pieces accidently landed inside the right passenger seat of the Cutlass Supreme. We kept on playing not realizing what happened. A few minutes later, the gentleman who was the fireman approached us. He wasn't smiling and said, "Who threw cheese in my car?" All the kids stayed quiet. I bravely stepped forward and said, "I did. I'm sorry, sir," taking responsibility for my actions. The man looked at me and hit me real hard. Mind you, I was only seven years old and about sixty pounds soaking wet. The man must have been about thirty-five years old and probably weighed about two hundred pounds. He smacked me so hard that he left the impression of his hand on my face, sort of like the five fingers of death. I was in shock as were the others around me. I couldn't believe that the nice man had raised his hand and struck me.

I walked home slowly and tried to hide it from parents. My mom quickly noticed the bruising on my face and asked me, "What happened?" I told her what had occurred, and she called the police. My dad wanted to confront the man and take matters into his own hands. Mom said, "No, let the law deal with him." The police came to our home and saw the bruise on my face and promptly arrested the man. He was taken out of his apartment in handcuffs, and I must admit, I felt rather sorry for him; but every time I looked in the mirror and gazed at my injury, I knew then and there that his punishment was justified. Yup.

36. Homeless, Fire, St. Charles Hotel, 1978

We were displaced after a fire in 1978. It was due to a space heater electrical wire malfunction. Space heaters were very popular back in the 1970s. They were cheap, flimsy, and poorly made. Many fires started due to the fact that many people kept their heaters too close to their beds at night. Blankets ignited, and homes burnt down. We lost all our belongings in the fire including a hundred-gallon fish tank. It was filled with all sorts of tropical fish. We ended up at a homeless shelter in Downtown Springfield. It was called the St. Charles Hotel. I thought the hotel was pretty cool. My cousins were also staying in the same hotel due to a fire as well. All of us used to run up and down the hallways like wild dogs in sheer pandemonium, playing tag or hide-and-seek.

We also ran or took the elevators down to the main lobby and constantly entered an Army-and-Navy store that was situated right next to the hotel. I loved that place. They had all sorts of War World II artifacts and memorabilia. It was astounding to say the least. Old helmets, shell casings, canteens, and bullets adorned the shop. Also army fatigues and dress wear were abundant for purchases. They had vintage brand gear such as PRO-Keds sneakers and Converse's Chuck Taylors. Buster Browns and Jelly Bean slippers could also be found in the store. We all wanted PRO-Keds, but we couldn't afford them. The store had some reject sneakers that resembled the Chuck Taylor's for an affordable price. The rejects had very thick bottoms, sort of like Frankenstein's shoes. All of us bought a pair for fifty cents each. We all looked like Herman Munster. We were the notorious Frankenstein gang.

We ran amok around the perimeter of the hotel to the dismay of all the guests. In the evenings, we retired to our rooms and watched *King Kong vs. Godzilla*, *Mothra*, *Gamera*, etc. We also watched lots of mystery movies. *Star Trek* was one our favorite tv shows as well. During bedtime, the iron steam radiators came on, and the room temperature soared. Everyone in the hotel sizzled from the heat. It was like the Bahamas. The water from the pipes gushed through the radiator like a geyser. We used towels to try and sustain the water and steam. We also tried opening the windows to stay cool, but it just didn't work. Welcome to the tropics. He-he.

There was a Greyhound bus depot across the street from the hotel. They had a large cafeteria that served the local patrons. Homeless families from the hotel were given free meals daily, which included breakfast, lunch, and dinner. For breakfast, the cafeteria offered pancakes, waffles, french toast, eggs and bacon, and all types of cereal. Tea, coffee, and orange juice were on the menu too. For lunch, they had a dazzling array of sandwiches. In the evening, they served mash potatoes with gravy and meat loaf, fried chicken with rice, spaghetti and meatballs, burgers and fries, and other treats. Cakes and pies were served for dessert. We ate to our hearts' delight, thanks to the generosity of the American Red Cross. After a few weeks, we left the hotel and were able to rebuild our lives. Yup.

37. Drugs in School, 1978

Drug use in American society was very common in the 1970s. I've witnessed firsthand the abuse of drugs within my own community, whether it was some teenager smoking a joint or heroin addicts with rubber bands tightly wrapped around their arms so that they could fully expose their veins to needles. Drugs were a major problem. You could find junkies laid out on the streets, alleyways, and stairwells, etc. They were flying higher than kites and had no cares in the world.

So many lives were ruined because of drug use. I've personally witnessed cocaine abuse as well. I remember drug users dicing cocaine laid on a small mirror with a razor blade, then taking a hit, snorting line after line of cocaine with a small straw into their nostrils. Even as a young child, I knew something was odd with this type of behavior. Potheads were found smoking in hallways, backyards, street corners, and wherever else they could light up. I hated the smell of marijuana and still do! It smelled like the potheads were smoking horse shit. Disgusting! Drug dealers peddled their wares on every street corner. *Dime bags, nickel bags, cheeba, periko,* etc.—these were some of the names given to the evil items the dealers were hustling on the streets. Walking to school early in the mornings, I often witnessed very young kids gathered on the street sniffing on a bag of glue. They took turns as each one sniffed his life away. I found this very bizarre and appalling. Sadly, some of the children were as young as six and seven years old. I thank God for giving me the strength to avoid such temptations in my own personal life. Amen!

38. Martial Arts Movies, Kung Fu Fever, 1978

In the 1970s, our family went to the movies a few times a month. *Kung Fu Fever* was in its heyday. Bruce Lee died in 1973, yet movie theaters were still playing his films to sold out audiences. Luckily for me, my parents really enjoyed the chop-socky movies of this era.

The first film I can remember seeing was in the early 1970s had the film's hero fighting against a tiger. Unfortunately, I can't recall the name of the film. Two films I did remember are *3 Evil Masters* (Shaw Brothers) and *Blood of the Dragon* (Jimmy Wang Yu). The fight scenes were awesome. One scene in *3 Evil Masters* that stuck in my head was the scene where the old master whips his hair around like a weapon, also the scene in *Blood of the Dragon* where Wang Yu sat on trees eating fruit before engaging in fights.

I snacked all the time while watching the chop-socky films of the era. I snacked on popcorn, Raisinets, and Coca-Cola. They were all part of my movie experience back then. Watching these films lit a fire underneath my seat. A fire that still burns today, which is an immense passion foe martial arts whether it's learning, practicing, or teaching them.. I want to thank my parents for planting the seeds of martial arts in my head by taking me to the kung fu cinema. Waya!

39. Haircut, 1978

Mom used to take Edward and me for haircuts every two months or so. We always got cool pushbacks (DAs). This haircut was very popular with boys in the 1970s. Many girls had Doobie doos (beehives). Haircuts were really cheap back then. The total cost for both of our haircuts was a paltry five bucks.

After getting the trim, I remember feeling supersharp and slick. I put both thumbs up in the air and cheerily said, "Ay!" just like Arthur Fonzarelli, better known as the Fonz on the *Happy Days* TV show. He had a slick pushback. John Travolta also had one on the *Saturday Night Fever* movie. He also showed off his DA in the *Welcome Back, Kotter* TV show, where he played Brooklyn high schooler Vinnie Barbarino. These two gentlemen were pop icons for the 1970s generation. Many kids wanted to be like them.

As we got a bit older, Mom felt it was time for us to start learning how to travel on our own. We journeyed the route to the barber with her many times before, but this time, we were doing it all alone. Mom wanted us to be more independent. I was eight years old, and my brother was eleven. Of course, him being the older sibling, she decided to put him in charge. I was very young and very stubborn, a total hardhead.

Early one Sunday afternoon, she gave us bus fare and money for us to both get our haircuts. Before we left our house, Mom looked at me in the eyes and said, "Listen to your big brother and do as he tells you and make sure you tip." Unfortunately for me, it went on deaf ears. We took the bus to the barber without a hitch. After we got our haircuts, we paid the barber five dollars. Each individual cut was only $2.50. We also gave him a two-dollar tip, a dollar for each one of us.

I looked at myself in the long mirror and dusted all the extra hair off my clothes. I felt sharper than a blade. I smiled widely into the mirror. My brother said, "We have to go. It's getting late." We both left the barbershop, and Edward said, "The bus stop is over here."

I scoffed at him and ignorantly replied, "No, it's not. The bus is on the other side!" My brother warned me that I'd get lost. *What that hell does he know?* I thought. "I'm going this way!" I said out loud.

My brother responded, "Okay, see you later!"

I didn't need him. I knew what I was doing. "Goodbye!" I shouted. My brother got on the bus and left. Just like that.

I saw his bus getting smaller and smaller as it drove into the distance, and then, it was gone. Shoot, I was all alone. *What if I was wrong?* I thought. It was still light out, but it was getting dark soon. I was about to learn a very good lesson: follow Mom's directions. I became angry and irritated. "I'll show that stupid face!" I angrily said to myself. I waited and waited as the sun started setting. I got nervous after a while. Finally, the darn bus arrived. I quickly hopped on. I felt bad for Edward. "He must be lost all alone somewhere," I imagined.

So the bus was speeding across the city, and now the streets started look foreign to me. It was pitch-black dark outside. "Where was I?" I worried. Fear overcame me. I felt the tears welling up inside my eyes. I tried being optimistic and containing my emotions. It was of no use. I started wailing in the back of the bus. The tears fell like a mighty rainstorm in a tropical rainforest with no end in sight. The bus driver reached the last stop and told me, "Hey, kid, this is the last stop!" I freaked out. The bus driver tried calming me down and called the authorities.

The police arrived and asked me several questions. They asked me my age, address, phone number, and my parents' names. Luckily for me, Mom had trained me and Edward at a very young age to memorize all this information in case we ever got lost. I couldn't contain myself. I kept crying hysterically. The cops reassured me, "Don't worry, we'll find your parents." Moments later, my parents and Edward arrived. Mom hugged me but scolded me as well and said sternly, "Always listen to your older brother." Lesson learned. Yup!

40. Fireworks Accident, 1978

Edward and I spent many weekends at my aunt Juanita's house. After suffering a fire a few months earlier, she relocated her family to some nice housing projects in Westfield, Massachusetts. We had a ball playing with our cousins Michelle, Raymond, and Debbie over the weekends, staying up late at night playing board games or watching TV. We also spent a lot of time cooling off in the local swimming pool. A nearby summer school program gave out free breakfast and lunch to needy, hungry, underprivileged kids in the neighborhood.

We took advantage of every opportunity to get some free chow. Breakfast was usually a bowl of milk and cereal and orange juice while lunch was a tasty bologna with cheese sandwich and a side of fruit with apple juice. We stuffed our faces with the grub.

We ran up and down the grassy hills that surrounded the homes in the area, even when it rained outside in the hot summer afternoons. One day, it rained only on one side of the block while the other side was dry. We dashed back and forth from one side to another, singing in the rain, just like the dance legend Gene Kelly. Afterward, a lovely, magnificent rainbow appeared in the sky overhead. We all stopped dancing in amazement and took it all in. We spent many hours play-ing in the housing projects of Westfield. We partook in all types of games. Most neighborhood kids rode their bikes while others roll-er-skated. Growing up during these years were awesome. There were no video games, computers, internet, or cell phones to distract us. Just plain old fun.

During the July Fourth season, you could purchase fireworks on the street from anyone—firecrackers, sparklers, jumping jacks, and even cherry bombs. Boys were mischievous with their newfound toys. Some rowdy boys stuck firecrackers into anthills, blasting them into kingdom come. Yet others stuck them into bottles, causing them to shatter into bits, resulting with a magnificent explosion. This was all in the sake of fun. Boys were always pushing the envelope, always trying to get away with what they could. Boys will be boys! I made the mistake of lighting a firecracker and holding it between my fin-gers. Bad mistake! It exploded and made a loud ringing sound in my ears. My fingers were ashy white with gunpowder residue. The sharp pain ran down my hand, and reminded me for several minutes there-after, of my foolishness.

There was one young boy who tried raising the bar. He had a bag of cherry bombs. Mind you, cherry bombs were very dangerous and yielded a much higher explosive than a normal firecracker. One afternoon while inside his home, the young boy lit a cherry bomb on the kitchen stove. He quickly tried to open the window and throw it out. The window was locked. The cherry bomb exploded in his hand. Unfortunately, the young victim lost three fingers on his right hand. The next day, he ran around the neighborhood with his hand bandaged up and played with all the kids as if nothing had ever happened. Yup!

41. Halloween, 1978

One of my favorite times of the year as a kid was Halloween. As a young child, this was an exhilarating experience. On Halloween day in 1978, my brother Edward and I wore *Star Wars* costumes. I was Chewbacca, and my brother was Darth Vader. The masks were very flimsy. They were made with cheap paint and plastic and attached with staples and a small rubber band to the back of the head. Mom took us to Baystate West in Downtown Springfield for a party and trick-or-treating. We had loads of fun. When we got back home, Mom always made sure that the candy was safe to eat. She checked to see if there were any injection sites for poison or if the wrappers were loose. She threw out any apples or fruit of any kind. The 1970s was a very dangerous and tumultuous time for trick-or-treaters due to the fact that some unsuspecting kids had razor blades placed in their apples and were seriously injured.

The movie *Halloween* had just come out. It was the talk of the town. Our parents took us to see it. We were always going out on the weekends to see the latest films. Our family were movie buffs. I had seen horror films prior to this one. But this movie was on another level. It truly scared the hell out of me. My heart raced as I began sweating uncontrollably. The music was utterly terrifying. We watched it in a small local theater with the red curtains that drew back. The theater also had gothic statues and candelabras that were attached to the walls surrounding the movie house. It was an extremely dark and eerie place, which in turn added to my fear. People shrieked in the audience every time Michael Myers slayed his victims with a loud and pulsating thud. Screams erupted throughout the movie theater. It was a roller coaster of emotions. The movie was a true masterpiece and became an instant classic. I had nightmares for weeks after. Yup.

42. First Karate Lesson, 1978

I trained in my first dojo in 1978. I watched a few classes from the outside of other dojos, but it was my first time actually participating in a class. Ironically, a bully named Ecki, whom I had fought with on several occasions, began his training with me. On a cold winter afternoon, a van with a karate emblem painted on its side drove into our neighborhood. They were promoting a karate school nearby. The karate guys gave permission slips to all the riffraff in the neighborhood. It was for some free classes. A couple of neighborhood kids got permission from their parents to attend the program, including Ecki and I.

It was snowing that evening, and the ground was slippery. We all hopped over a puddle of slush in order to enter the van. Regardless, our feet got drenched. The ride to the school was eerily quiet. We were packed in the van like sardines. *Where the hell are we going?* I thought. We finally reached our destination, and everyone hopped out of the van. We entered a large building, and then all boarded an elevator. It was the quietest elevator ride of my life. The door opened on the fourth floor. Right then and there, I got my first impression of a real dojo: the stench of sweaty feet! The carpet reeked! It was musky in the dojo.

The silence was broken when one of the black belts harshly barked out some commands. "Get off the elevator and take off your shoes!" I said to myself, "No way, man!" A few kids started talking and complaining. Some other rough and tough black belts joined in and yelled, "Hurry up!" We all quickly did as we were instructed. We joined a class already in session made up mostly of adult black belts and brown belts. They had us run, jump, drop down for push-ups, and basically tortured us with drills. "Kiai, kiai, kiai!" we all shouted in unison. No one complained. We didn't want to get our asses kicked. So we endured the workout. It was like the scene right out of *Enter the Dragon* where Jim Kelly visited his old dojo. Toward the end of the class, we started learning some self-defense techniques. "Now this is cool," I whispered to a kid nearby.

When I got home, I tried my new moves on my brother and almost kicked him out of the second-floor window. He wasn't smiling. Sorry, bro. Kung fu fever! Waya!

43. DeBerry School, Boston, 1976

I attended DeBerry School in Springfield, Massachusetts, in 1976. I was in the second grade. My teacher was Mrs. Davis. One afternoon, she planned a tourist trip for our class to visit Boston. All the kids boarded a Greyhound bus as we embarked into the unknown. It was a three-hour ride. Some kids played on the bus while others took naps. After a long and arduous drive, we finally arrived at our destination. We cheered as we entered the city.

Our first stop was Fenway Park, the home of the notorious Red Sox. I was a New Yorker and a die-hard Yankees fan, but it was cool to see the stadium nevertheless. We also visited the majestic Prudential Tower, which at the time was the tallest skyscraper in Boston. It was terrifying as we took the elevator up and made our way to the top floor. Looking out from the large windows and gazing down on all the people from above made my stomach crawl. They were the size of ants. After our gravity-defying experience, we exited the building and then made our way over to the aquarium. This was my favorite part of the trip. They had all types of fishes and sea urchins. It reminded me of my dad's hundred-gallon fish tank at home loaded with all variety of fishes. My favorite exhibit bar none was the shark tank. I had just seen *Jaws* at the movie theater and was very afraid yet totally intrigued by the underwater predators. It was great to see them swimming and splashing about without taking a bite out of some unsuspecting victim.

We had tons of fun. It was now time to reboard the bus for lunch. Everyone brought their own food in paper bags or in lunch boxes. I sat back down in my seat, ready to eat the meal that Mom had prepared for me. She made several sandwiches and added a bag of chips with a soda on the side as well. Everyone munched away on their food, including Mrs. Davis and the bus driver. After lunch, the kids became restless and played around on the bus. Mrs. Davis told everyone to sit still until she returned from doing an errand outside. The bus driver watched over us when she left. This was our cue to act up and misbehave. We bounced around, cracked jokes, and talked about our splendid day. I was thirsty at this point but ran out of soda. Mrs. Davis left her new soda unattended. It was lying on the seat inside her purse. One of my so-called friends dared me to open it and take a sip. He said, "Go ahead. I won't tell!" All the other kids joined in and said the same. I was like, "Yeah, I'm very thirsty. I'm going to take a sip, and why not?" I worked my way around the seat and slowly grabbed the bottle from her purse. I opened it and took the most delicious gulp of soda ever. "Ahh!" I said after my excursion into the place of no return. I felt good! There was a deep silence on the bus, and then it happened. "Ooh, I'm telling!" could be heard all over the bus. *Yikes!* I thought. The second Mrs. Davis entered the bus, all the kids ratted me out. Traitors. My face was tomato red from the sheer embarrassment. Mrs. Davis reprimanded me and told me, "You owe me fifty cents!" When we arrived back at the school, she told my parents about the incident. I was punished for my naughty deed. The next day, I returned to school with the fifty cents and returned it to Mrs. Davis in front of the whole class. It was very humiliating ordeal. Moral of the story: never trust kids on a school bus. Ha ha. Yup!

44. Falling off a Roof, 1978

I was always a very hyperactive child. I was never on Ritalin. It was a very popular drug prescribed for kids by their doctors in the 1970s. It helped youngsters calm their nerves and settle them down. Under the influence of the drug, the kids became like the vegetables in *One Flew over the Cuckoo's Nest* film. Mom wasn't an advocate for its usage. Well, anyway, I continued being mischievous day in and day out and getting myself into fixes. Like most kids in the 1970s, we spent a good portion of our time playing outside. We played street games, rode bikes, built clubhouses, climbed trees, climbed walls, climbed fences, played on the street, played in the fire hydrant, played on the fire escape, etc. We had an abundance of energy. We didn't sit at home all day long fidgeting with our fingers. Nope. We were out and about.

Spending so much time outdoors had its benefits, but also many risks. Many hospital emergency rooms were flooded with children being attended to for cuts, bruises, bumps, and broken bones. I, too, had my fair share of accidents. My first mishap occurred when I was two years old; of course, I was too young to recall, but Mom remembered all too well. She said that while playing, I'd fallen down a long flight of stairs. My head was split wide open, and blood spurted out at an alarming rate. Mom yelled terrified, "Please someone help! Please help! call an ambulance!" A young man, a good Samaritan, heard my mother's plea for help and quickly scooped me up and carried me for blocks running as fast as he possibly could toward the hospital. Mom was right behind him in tears, crying frantically as we arrived at the ER. The doctors quickly rushed me in and stitched me up. The man had disappeared, nowhere to be found. He must've been my guardian angel. Mom was eternally grateful, and so was I.

One night in 1978, my cousins and I gathered on a rooftop to play. It was a normal thing for kids to do such things back then. One on my cousins placed a wooden plank between the ledge of our roof and the adjoining roof. All of us started crossing one by one. Luck would have it that I was the last to cross. I unfortunately missed my footing and plunged headfirst into the darkness below. I hit the bottom with a loud crashing thud. I got up with many bruises all over my face and was drenched in blood. I cried in pain as my cousins walked me back home. I broke my nose and several teeth in the fall. I was rushed by ambulance to the nearest hospital. I had several reconstructive oral and nasal surgeries soon after that. I was only seven at the time. Yup.

45. Hit by a Car, 1978

One summer afternoon, while playing ball in the street, my cousin David from Jersey City was tragically hit by a car. I was back home in Springfield at the time. My brother was visiting David's house for a week in New Jersey. This is my brother Edward's account of what occurred that day.

A bunch of neighborhood kids were playing on the sidewalk. My cousin ran after a ball that rolled onto the street between two parked cars. As he reached out for the ball, a car simultaneously sped down the street and hit him square in the face with the front fender, shattering his jaw. My cousin fell underneath the car. He was afraid of getting run over by the tires. So he grabbed on to the car's muffler to escape further harm and in doing so was burned very badly.

The driver was unaware that he hit someone and actually thought he ran over a cardboard box. My brother, bearing witness to the tragedy, quickly took off and ran to the nearest supermarket. My aunt Ana (David's mother) was paying for groceries on the cashier's line. My brother burst into the supermarket and told her the bad news. She threw everything in the air and ran out of the store in a frenzy. My cousin was rushed to the local hospital. He was treated for second- and third-degree burns all over his body. The doctors made him gain weight so that he could have skin grafts done. He also needed to have his jaw realigned. He was in the hospital for two months. He received treatment many years thereafter. Today he is fine, minus a few scars. Thank goodness.

46. Street Fight, on the Move, 1979

The year was 1979. I was nine years old. My family was relocating into a new home. We started moving early in the morning. My cousins Vicki, Chuito, and Willie helped us out. All of us including Mom and Edward, lifted and hoisted very heavy furniture all day long. By midafternoon, we were totally spent. Exhausted. Dad unfortunately was not present to help us. He was incarcerated and doing time in the city jail.

All of us loaded the family car with furniture and our personal belongings. Mom had a Pinto. It was a very small car. Fortunately, we were able to cram everything inside it. As we were about to leave, a young lady and an older woman approached the vehicle. They both yelled and hurled insults at us and became overly aggressive. It was our next-door neighbors Aleda and Elizabeth. They were the mother and sister of a neighborhood bully named Ecki, whom I fought against several times. Ecki also had an older brother named Pancho. Pancho was the first guy I've ever seen up rocking, a.k.a. Brooklyn Rock, which was a dance performed by gang members. Pancho was a really cool guy who dated my cousin Vicki. The big problem was that Elizabeth and Vicki couldn't stand each other.

A confrontation was inevitable. A few words were exchanged between them, and all hell broke loose. It was like cats and dogs. The fur started flying. Punches in bunches! Yup! The fight was epic. King Kong versus Godzilla. Ali versus Frazier. The girls went at it. At one point in the exchange, Vicki started getting the upper hand and besting Elizabeth. She nailed her in the face with several unanswered blows. Blam, blam! Aleda tried to rescue her daughter and intervened by pulling Vicki's blouse off. My mother jumped in and pounced on Aleda. Mom clobbered her with several punches. Now it was a tag team match courtesy of four pissed off women.

All the boys watched on the sidelines without interfering. I couldn't believe the spectacle that had unfolded before us. I pinched myself and thought, *This can't be real.* It was a full-scale battle royal. Punches, scratches, pushing, shoving, and finally, it was over. A few more parting insults and the women went their separate ways. Pancho showed up but said nothing. It was a woman's quarrel. Mom and Vicki licked their wounds, and we kept moving as if nothing had happened. A day in the life of a child. Yup.

47. No Speak Any English, 1979

I often heard my parents speaking of Martin Luther King, John F. Kennedy, and of social unrest. They were keenly aware of the social conditions in our country at that time—racism, bigotry, discrimination, unemployment, inflation, crime, poverty, and a wide array of other issues that plagued our nation. Our parents taught my brother and me, from a very young age, that when we were confronted with racism, to keep our heads high and not be discouraged. This wasn't always so easy for young Puerto Rican kids growing up in the '70s.

One day, while attending school in the third grade, I was thoroughly reprimanded and embarrassed by my teacher. I was caught speaking in Spanish to my friend. She pointed me out and had me stand in front of the whole class and, in a very loud tone said, "Speak English only. You're in America!" I was so humiliated and felt very ashamed. As soon as I got home, I told my parents about my bad day at school. My parents were livid. Mom emphatically said, "Tomorrow, speak Spanish at school all day. You're Puerto Rican. And never forget who you are!" I felt a sense of beaming pride come over me.

The next day, I went to school defiant as ever. My teacher was shocked and in dismay as I spoke Spanish with a huge grin on my face. When she tried to hush me, I blurted out loud and told her blatantly, "I'm Puerto Rican, and I'll speak Spanish as I wish!" The room went silent. My classmates watched in disbelief. She quickly jumped out of her seat and escorted me by the hand to the principal's office. I ruffled her feathers, and boy, did it feel good. Yup. Growing up as a Latino wasn't always smooth sailing. I'm fairly light skinned, but my mother and relatives are on the dark side (African roots). I was very well spoken and had no problem communicating. I had several White friends growing up, so racism toward me was never really an issue. I was treated respectfully for the most part. However, my parents were another story. I recall searching for apartments with Edward and Mom and having doors slammed in our faces. Landlords yelled, "No Blacks or Puerto Ricans!"

"What? Unbelievable!" I said to myself. I was totally shocked and appalled. My heart sank. *How could they treat us this way? It was so unfair and unjustified,* I thought. I felt so much pain for my parents. They struggled so much with this type of mistreatment and condemnation. Yup.

48. United Skates of America, 1979

One of the best times we ever had growing up as kids was going to the franchise United Skates of America. This was during the late '70s and early '80s. My brother and I loved to roller-skate. We both had skates and trailblazed the neighborhood with them, but USA was a totally different experience. They had a huge skating rink with disco lights, music, DJ, snack bar, games, and hundreds of skaters grooving to the beat, swerving and swirling to the Jackson 5, the Bee Gees, Kool and the Gang, the Doobie Brothers, Earth, Wind & Fire, etc. It was epic. Unfortunately, due to the dwindling numbers of skaters, most rinks closed down during the mid- and late '80s. Lately, there has been a nostalgic resurgence to skating once again. Young and old can be found speeding around roller rinks all over the world, grooving to classic music. So if you were ever bored and needed some excitement, look up your local skating rink and have yourself the time of your life. Yup.

49. A Child Named Bially, 1980

As I mentioned earlier, I was born in the Bronx, New York. The name on my birth certificate read Bially Sanchez. My mother once told me that the inspiration for that name came to her during a dream. As a young child, I was very fond of it.

As the years passed by, I met many other kids with standard everyday names like John, Michael, Rob, Carlos, Henry, Susan, Diana, Greg, Chris, Raymond, etc. A large variety of names. Never once did I meet or even heard of another kid named Bially. I was like, "What the hell!" One day, while coming home from school, I was shocked when my brother said, "You see that kid over there. His name is Bially too." I couldn't believe it. How could this be possible? I looked at him up and down in awe. It was surreal.

Most of the time, Edward and I got along well, but like most normal siblings, sometimes, we had our quarrelsome moments. We made fun of each other. I nicknamed him George Washington. I felt his hairdo was shaped like the first president's image on the dollar bill. One day, out of anger, he said, "You're named after a bagel!" What he actually meant to say was a bialy. It's a pastry found in most Italian bakeries. He teased me for many years.

I eventually became very disenchanted with my name and felt rather embarrassed every time someone said it. I reached a point where I wanted to change my name. I begged my parents constantly to have it changed. Tired of hearing me whine and complain, they finally obliged. My parents went through all the court proceedings to give me a fresh, new start. I finally said goodbye to Bially and hello to Anthony, a name I personally chose myself. The year was 1980. Many years have passed. I must say that I was now okay with being called Bially by my relatives or loved ones. After all, my mom very lovingly christened me with that name, and that was surely nothing to be ashamed off. Yup!

50. My Uncle Paul, 1980s

My uncle Paul was born in Puerto Rico in 1956. He was the youngest of twenty kids. My mother was the second youngest of the group. Her name was Paula and she is four years older than my uncle. My uncle lived with Grandma in the Bronx. When she decided to up and move to Springfield, Massachusetts, he decided to stay put in the Bronx.

My uncle was an avid young boxer and competed in the NYC Golden Gloves tournament. He attended Morris High School. He was also a member of the high school track team and competed in many races across the city, most notably in the Van Cortlandt Park meets. My uncle amassed many trophies and awards throughout the years.

Art was one of his favorite hobbies. I must admit he had a knack for it. He had many sketch books filled with his drawings all over the apartment. He was also a very crafty chess player. I saw him partake in many matches against my dad and several others. He played for many hours over a hot cup of coffee.

My uncle used to tell me many stories about gangs and crime back then. He mentioned Morris High School (a.k.a. Mars) and some of the gangs that ravaged the neighborhood, such as the Tomahawks and the Ghetto Brothers. He never joined a gang because he was too busy with boxing and track training and his schoolwork, doing his best to get out of the ghetto, which he eventually did. My uncle wanted to be a doctor as a gift for his mother, but when my grandmother passed away, my uncle lost his focus on his studies. Eventually, he refocused and went to college and today is a registered nurse.

My uncle Pablito worked as a lifeguard at Orchard Beach in the summers of the 1970s and 1980s. He was very popular among his friends and the ladies. In the early 1980s, he hosted house parties with a live DJ. These gatherings took place at least once a month in his apartment. The parties were held on University Avenue near Fordham Road. Our family always attended his popular get-togethers.

During the party, Edward and I skipped out for some pizza. The pizzeria was right around the corner. Fifty-cent slices. The slices were scrumptious. After indulging ourselves, we then proceeded to hang out at a local park. We rode the swings, played on the slides and seesaws, and basically just goofed around. We soon returned to the party. By the time we got back, the party had really started jumping off. The apartment was packed, and everyone was dancing to the early radio hits of the 1980s—"Heartbeat," "Last Night a DJ Saved My Life," "Jump to It," "I Remember What You Like," Don't Stop Till You Get Enough," etc.

My brother and I entertained ourselves by jumping on my uncle's waterbed, hoping not to bust it. We also listened to his new Sony Walkman. We had fun partying with the adults, but after a certain time, it was off to sleep—well, at least for me. Edward kept partying. Yup.

51. Poison Ivy, 1980

Kids from the '70s and '80s generation loved to play outside. We always had to make sure that we completed our homework assignments in a timely fashion. Our daily chores around our home had to be finished as well before we could leave the house. Once we were free to roam outside, we explored the neighborhood for some fun and occasional mischief. We really loved climbing trees and digging into the ground, looking for all sorts of creepy, crawly bugs. Most boys and a few tomgirls did these types of things. I always liked to play in the bushes. I enjoyed hiding and jumping out of the darkness to scare the other unsuspecting kids. I spent some time roaming about in the forest as well. I was allergic to a wide array of things back then such as pears, apples, plums, peaches, strawberries, walnuts, cashews, almonds, beans, shrimp, dust, pollen, and many types of plants, etc.

One summer afternoon, I spent some time frolicking in the forest. I ran amok, zipping my way past every bush and branch that I could find. As I exited the forest, I noticed some strange rashes on my arms and legs. I quickly went home to wash up. I took a bath, but the rash persisted and had now spread to my face. My nose was very swollen and was now twice its normal size. I looked like a dwarf. My parents took me to the hospital. I felt all eyes glaring at me as we entered the emergency room. People looked at me like I was an outcast. I felt strange and confused and extremely itchy. The doctor took a long, hard stare at me as he brought me into a room for an examination. His prognosis was that I had a severe case of poison ivy. He prescribed some cream and antibiotics for the rash. That was the end of me playing in the bushes. Yup.

52. Chicken Delight, 1980

We lived on 103 Wolcott Street in Springfield, Massachusetts, for a brief moment in 1980. We moved into a small house that was owned and rented by a Polish couple. The house was more like a cottage, made mostly of brick with an attic and a basement. It had a large side and backyard. My brother and I shared a room. It was nice and comfortable. I really liked it. It was a very beautiful home.

My parents bought furnishings for our new pad—a living room set, dining room set, bedroom set, television, and stereo set. They adorned the walls of our home with pictures and decorations. My brother and I had our room filled with toys. We had bunk beds. I was smaller, so I slept on the top bunk. We also had a black-and-white TV in our room. We had a wire hanger wrapped in aluminum foil as an antenna for better reception. The buttons usually fell off, so we'd change the channels with a screwdriver or pliers. We always had to mess around with the vertical and horizontal control buttons.

The attic also had some of our belongings and toys—really cool and sleek racing tracks (Tyco), Stretch Armstrong rubber dolls, Evel

Knievel toys, Twister, electric train sets, and plastic army men. We also had Superman, Spiderman, and Batman and Robin action figures, the Incredible Hulk muscle set, the Six Million–Dollar Man action figure, *Jaws* game, etc. We played up there for hours.

We also played in the basement. It was very dark and dingy, not surprising. My dad kept his movie projector and work tools down there. Our family had a dog, chicken, and a rooster, which we kept in a cage in the basement. The chicken laid her eggs, which eventually hatched, producing the cutest little chicklings. They were so adorable. I fed them and gave them water daily. I'd let them out into the backyard for fresh air. Our dog mingled with the chickens, though often chased by the rooster. I loved my pets. They meant everything to me.

One day, I arrived home from school early. I was sadly informed by my parents that our happy little chicken went missing. "How could this be? They were all locked up in their cages," I suspiciously replied.

Mom said, "Maybe she got lost and ran into the neighbor's yard."

I looked in the neighbor's yard, but nothing. *How far could she go*, I thought. I looked all over frantically, but I couldn't find her. I lost hope and finally gave up the search.

Later that night, we were all seated at the dinner table, and the food smelled really good. I was very worried and unhappy about my pet. "Maybe I'll feel better after I eat," I assumed. Well, just maybe. Edward and I set the table for supper. Mom started serving us rice and beans, vegetables, and finally, the delectable main course: the roasted chicken. Huh! A look of gloom crossed my face. I was totally dumbfounded. Perplexed. In the twilight zone.

Mom didn't utter a word, but my brother and dad knew very well what had transpired. My eyes tightened. My nose flared. My breathing became shallow. My family very nonchalantly consumed the bird (chicken) as if nothing had happened, licking their fingers with wide grins on their faces. Disgusting! I felt like puking. These crazy people. "Who are you? I must be adopted," I grumbled to myself. "How can you do such a thing." I just sat there watching in agony, yuck!

After this tragedy, I resumed my normal routine, playing in the attic, basement, and the yard. Sometimes our family visited an elderly woman who lived next door. She reminded me of the queen, Elizabeth. She was very sweet. She served us tea with cookies every time we dropped by. She always commented on how well-mannered my brother and I were. "Such good manners," she softly said. Mom always smiled with delight. She was very keen on good manners and respect for elders, but in the back of my head, I was still thinking about my poor pet. Yup!

53. Evel Knievel on the Bike Ramp, 1980

On bright summer days, we'd take out our bikes for a ride. I had a black and blue cool Huffy and my brother had a ten speed. Most times, Edward would take off on his bike and just disappear. I, on the other hand, would join my friends in the park. We usually set up a ramp just like the one Evel Knievel jumped on TV, but much smaller in dimensions, of course. We also wanted to be daredevils.

Most kids loved Evel Knievel and wanted to be just like him. The Fonz character from the *Happy Days* TV show was also popular among the kids for his motorcycle skills. In one episode, the Fonz jumped over some sharks on his bike. On one particular day, my friends and I setup a ramp, but this was no normal ramp. We stacked a large mountain of bricks underneath it. It was a super ramp. No one else attempted to jump this monstrosity. I so valiantly stepped forward and volunteered. I was very brave and had nerves of steel, but on the other hand, I was very foolish to attempt it.

All my friends stood on the sidelines as I revved up my bike from a distance. Vroom! I had the ramp on my radar and took off. I started pedaling faster and faster as my heart raced, and my friends watched in awe of what was to come. The ramp got closer and closer as a lined up my bike with it. With the scalding sun overhead, I could see the shadow of my motorcycle on the pavement—well, my so-called motorcycle. At least that was how I imagined it. I could feel the wind brushing against my face as I gained more speed. Finally, I felt my front tire pressed up on the ramp as a feeling of elation filled me. But that moment was short-lived as I noticed my rear tire skid off the ramp, and my handlebar turned abruptly counterclockwise.

At this point, I was in midflight and knew that I was in deep trouble. I caught a quick glimpse of my friends' faces as they stood in astonishment. I landed with no control whatsoever of my bike. I flew over it and landed on the hot pavement face first. I slid a few feet as my facial skin peeled off like hot butter. I also peeled off a few layers of skin off my arms. I could feel the heat of the blazing sun beaming off the cement. I got up in a hurry and looked over at my bike and then realized the magnitude of my injuries. I started shrieking and wailing as the pain set in. I looked over at my buddies with their mouths agape, shocked in disbelief. I looked the part of a character out of a horror movie.

My friends helped me pick up my bike and escorted me home. My parents quickly rushed me to the hospital. The doctor gave me a wonderful tetanus shot and disinfected my wounds. He also gave me a prescription for antibiotics. Another fun filled day in the park. Yup.

54. Handball Fight, 1980

A few days after breaking my arm, I found myself playing on a jungle gym and monkey bars in a nearby park. I was playing and goofing off with some of my buddies. They all signed my cast for me. Edward was in the local schoolyard nearby, playing handball with three of his friends, or so-called friends.

A few minutes later, from the corner of my eye, I quickly caught a glimpse of Edward wrestling with his three pals. I squinted, trying to get a closer look. I observed them very carefully and realized that many punches were being thrown and all in my brother's direction. "Hold up, they ain't wrestling. They're jumping my brother. What the fuck!" I said as I jumped of the bars. I raced over to my brother faster than the Flash.

Edward was fighting all three of them, so I jumped in. My brother was in a headlock as the other punks punched him in his back. *Fuck that! Time for revenge!* I thought, angered. I leaped in the air and cracked one sucker in the head with my cast. He let my brother go. I attacked the others from behind and proceeded to pounce on them with my cast. That was the break Edward needed as he dismantled them one by one with his fists by punching their lights out. He punched the last guy in the face and said, "Now give me my fucking handball!"

We were Batman and Robin that day. We sure kicked some ass. I yelled out at the punks as we left the schoolyard, "Don't mess with my bro!" Word up! The nerve of these punks. They tried snatching my brother's handball from him. Unbelievable. Yup.

55. Sijo Kalaii Griffin and the Iron Dragons, 1980

I've always believed in honoring those who have helped you on your journey through life. Respect for the knowledge and wisdom they may have imparted on you. I've had many great martial arts teachers along the way. My heart and mind are filled with wonderful memories of their teachings. I began my journey into martial arts in 1978.

I started my training in karate. My teachers were very strict. They were firm and no-nonsense individuals who took their art very seriously. In 1980, I started learning Kajukenbo (Kenpo) at the Iron Dragon Martial Art Studio. The head instructor was renowned martial arts expert Kalaii K. Griffin. He was a student of the legendary Ed Parker. Bruce Lee was first discovered at Ed Parker's Martial Arts event at the Long Beach Internationals in 1964. Bruce Lee later appeared on the *Green Hornet* TV show.

I attended martial arts classes every Saturday afternoon. Classes were only ten dollars a month. Priscilla was my instructor for the class. She wore a stars-and-stripes uniform. She yelled out, "Fudo-dachi!" She was a very good teacher. She told the students who attended the class to play some music when training at home for motivation. To this day, forty-plus years later, I could still remember her words. Sometimes, higher belts walked into the class, and I was left feeling awed. One kid in particular had a short marine buzz cut, highwater pants, and an American patch on his Gi. He reminded me of a young Chuck Norris.

Sometimes, I caught a glimpse of the black belts in training when I was waiting for my parents to pick me up. The black belts trained like it was War World III. It sounded like they were killing one another inside. Bam! Slam! Bam! The *sijo*, a.k.a. head instructor, Kalaii K. Griffin taught the class. He was very strict. I was very intrigued by his aura and presence. He was a very luminous and powerful presence at the dojo. When he was in the room, all eyes were on him. Everyone paid close attention. The dojo was at his command. The Iron Dragon Dojo. Chi'en.

56. Ghosts in the House, 1980

Living on 103 Wolcott Street was rather pleasant for the most part. But there were some rather strange happenings occurring after hours. Now mind you, I grew up spending my time watching horror movies on late night TV and at the drive-in movie theater. I had a very vivid imagination. I was extremely afraid of the dark. I always looked in the closet and peeked under my bed before going to sleep. Creepy sounds freaked me out at night.

Going to sleep in the darkness was an arduous task for me. Plus, my older brother was a practical joker. He scared the life out of me every chance he had. When we were lying asleep, he'd make groaning sounds from the bottom bunk or raise his hand between our bunkbeds and chant, "Chiller!" I jumped up from the top bunk and climbed down the wooden ladder attached to the bed frame and darted out of the room in a hurried mess toward my parents' room in tears. My brother belted out in laughter from the darkness, which consumed our sleeping quarters.

All the neighborhood kids would share ghost stories and tall tales of the macabre and eerie. My mind was full of all the supernatural mumble jumble I heard day-to-day. My nerves were rattled rather easily, and I walked on eggshells. I was startled by loud sounds or sudden movements. The house we lived in had a creepy window in the attic. Every time I played in the backyard, I would gaze up and imagine someone in the window peering back at me. That creepy window reminded me of *The Amityville Horror* movie.

One evening, as our family sat at the dinner table, we casually struck up a random conversation. My parents started the conversation off by sharing some of their experiences in the new home with us. The feeling at the dinner table became somber. Oh no, I felt it coming on—a ghost story! What I heard that night terrified the dickens out of me. Mom commenced by telling us that some nights, while she lay fast asleep, she could feel her blanket being pulled off. When she quickly turned to look at my dad, he was out cold. It occurred for several nights after. My brother looked startled. I unwittingly thought, *Mom must be losing her marbles*. Then Dad interjected, "I, too, was awoken in the middle of the night by the sound of someone dragging chairs against the attic floor."

"Really, Dad," I shrieked.

"Yes," he quickly replied. And he continued, "On another night, I slowly opened the basement door and could vividly hear someone sweeping the floor with a broom. I scurried to your bedroom, and you and your brother were on your third dreams. I raced back to the master bedroom, and your mother was snuggled in bed."

Holy crap, that was all I needed to hear. It confirmed my feelings about the house. We had ghosts!

A few days later, my parents stepped out to buy groceries. My brother was in the attic. I very reluctantly decided to go down into the cellar and check on our pets. I checked the birds' cages. I fed them all and gave them some fresh water to drink. I played with my beloved pets when suddenly, my face turned pale white. "No way. Impossible. It can't be," I whispered under my breath. Then I heard it again and again. It was "the sound of someone sweeping the floor with a broom." I dropped everything I was doing and tiptoed my behind out of there. I bumped into a few things during my hasty exit. When I reached the top of the stairs, I screamed out in a panic. My brother heard me yell out in fear and raced down from the attic to help but was too late. I crashed through the front screen door of our home just as our parents arrived in the family car. I was drenched in sweat. Boo-hoo! Yup.

57. Broken Arm, Wrestling, 1980

In 1980, I found myself playing with some friends at a housing project. We climbed and scaled a few fences and played tag and several other games. We all quickly got bored and decided to engage in some wrestling matches. I loved watching wrestling on TV with the likes of Bob Backlund, Bruno Sammartino, Pedro Morales, Tony Atlas, Ken Patera, André the Giant, Ivan Putski, and countless others.

I was a pretty strong ten-year-old kid and was able to out wrestle a couple of the boys. At one point, we all engaged in a melee, a free for all, every man for himself. So here I was in the middle of an open field, fully entangled with three other boys in a death match. Together, we formed the human octopus made up of eight arms, engulfed in an internal battle of might and wits. Sweat poured off our brows as we all panted in the hot and humid, scorching temperature. The unforgiving sun beamed down upon us from the clear and unadulterated blue sky. We all suddenly collapsed as the ground trembled beneath our feet. I was caught underneath as the boys landed on top of me like a stack of cards. I tried supporting all the extra weight with my right arm. I heard it snap like a twig, but ironically, I felt no pain whatsoever. The bunch of us quickly scrambled to our feet. I dusted myself off, and then I saw the wide-eye expression in the boys' eyes as I lifted my mangled arm. Again, like I said before, I felt no pain, but seeing my limb in that state, twisted and contorted, caused my tears to flow ever so freely. My arm snapped below the wrist, making my hand appear longer than it was.

I held on to my arm as I quickly galloped across the street. My parents were in the backyard of our home and heard my distant cries. My mom yelled out, "I told you so!" Hearing her words of reprimand made me shriek even louder. We got in the family car and took off to the hospital. When we arrived, they took X-rays and prepped me for a cast. I wore the cast for about two months. All my friends signed it with magic markers. The humidity caused my arm to itch irresistibly. I scratched it with whatever was handy—a ruler, wire hanger, pencil, whatever. I couldn't wait till this blasted thing came off. When it finally did, my arm looked skinny, frayed, and decrepit. When I got home, I quickly washed it and then ran outside to play. Back to normal. Yup.

Chapter 2 (1981–84)

58. Bad Times, Family, 1981

The year was 1981. It was a very tumultuous time for our family. Dad was out of work, and Mom was at her wits' end. We had no money for rent, clothes, and sadly, at certain times, food. We went to the local church pantries to get help with food and clothing. We also received help from the Salvation Army and, whenever possible, bought clothing at the Goodwill thrift store.

The food we graciously received from the pantries was not appealing at all—mostly canned creamed soup, canned hash browns, powdered milk, and baked beans. That never bothered me as a kid. What got under my skin was the constant bickering between my parents. It drove me up the wall. Dad fell heavily into drug use. Mom did her upmost best to keep our family together. She held part-time jobs and tried being creative with the little cash flow we had. Dad on the other hand was a slave to his habit and began deteriorating slowly. He worked in several auto body shops for cars here and there but was constantly being fired for being late or not showing up to work at all. Eventually, he set up shop in our backyard, working for pennies to support his drug abuse.

We had no choice but to go on welfare (public assistance). Eventually, the situation kept getting worse. The cupboards and fridge were empty. The apartment we lived in was frigid. Tempers were flaring. Edward and I had to get free breakfast and lunch at school. Dinner was the problem. Sometimes, we didn't have anything to eat at all. Very tough times! The fights with my parents became more intense. My dad became more irritable and shorter tempered. He lashed out at all of us. It was totally horrible, and I often cried. I was always worried about Mom and Edward. Dad was not the same man I remembered growing up as a young child. He was now Dr. Jekyll and Mr. Hyde. I had knots in my stomach. Yup.

59. Jersey City, 1981

We moved to Jersey City, New Jersey, at the end of 1980. I was ten years old. My brother was thirteen years old. We lived near Montgomery Avenue, a few blocks from the Jersey City Hospital. Our family moved into a small building. We lived on the third floor. The young superintendent looked Jewish or Russian. He had a thin handlebar mustache and always wore a cap just like the one Gilligan donned on the TV show.

My dad was out of work at the time. He had a couple of jobs lined up. He was in school training to drive tractor trailers. He was also learning auto body repair as well. We were on public assistance at the time. We received the minimal amount of help allotted. Food stamps helped us put meals on the table for the first few weeks of the month. I was so happy when it was time to make *la compra*. It was Spanish for "groceries." La Compra always fell on the first day of the month. Our family went to the local supermarket. As we entered the store, my brother and I made a beeline for the cereal aisle. We picked out our favorite boxes, one for each of us. We also snatched our favorite snacks, which for me, it was most indisputably a large bag of Doritos. My brother, on the other hand, went for the cookies, Chips Ahoy or the Keebler brand.

We indulged ourselves in our newfound fortune whenever possible, enjoying the glory of hot, cooked meals. During the last week of every month, we were basically out of food. Edward and I woke up extra early so that we could have breakfast in school. We ate lunch there too. Sometimes, when we got home, there was absolutely nothing to eat at all. If we were lucky enough, we found scraps in the fridge, but never enough for a complete meal. We filled our empty bellies with a jar of stale pickles and expired peanut butter. These were the only remnants left of a once-thriving refrigerator. The cupboards were bare, except for the mice droppings left by our uninvited guests. If we were fortunate enough to have a bowl of rice, we adorned it with the greasy meat remains of a dirty pan. Sometimes, I felt nauseous, not due to the food but to the lack thereof. At bedtime, my pillow caught my teardrops as they slithered down my face in my attempts to dream of something better.

Our apartment was pleasant during the spring, summer, and autumn months. Winter was the problem. There was no heat, and the apartment was freezing. There was seldom any hot water. And as a matter of fact, the hot water only lasted for about three or four minutes at a time. This was just enough time to fill the bathtub half-way. I submerged myself underwater in an effort to stay warm. As I came back up, I could plainly see the heat coming off my body. My breath was also visible in the frigid apartment. I hated this wretched place. "Why did we move here?" I cried as I shivered. "It is always fucking cold, damn it!" I said in angst. "Where the hell is Gilligan with his stupid hat, and why doesn't he fix this problem!" My parents made many attempts to have the problem resolved, even at one point getting the housing administration involved. But unfortunately, our complaints fell on deaf ears.

Though the apartment was a shithole. I must admit, we had an incredible panoramic view from our kitchen window of the Hudson River and lower Manhattan. The Twin Towers stood tall and grand. I was spellbound by their magnitude and sheer size. I gazed constantly out of the window at the towers. Oh, how I miss them (sad face). As the spring time approached, living in the apartment became more tolerable. Ironically, I spent a lot of time watching *Gilligan's Island* on TV. I watched *Woody Woodpecker* and *Bugs Bunny* before going to school in the morning, sometimes over a bowl of cereal with milk.

After school, I spent time with my Filipino buddies Rodman Ante and Thomas Lacy. They always gave me an ear to my problems and were very supportive. Cool friends. We all attended PS 17 on Duncan Hill Avenue. We usually studied at the library and walked home together. It was 1980, and we always said to one another, "The world will end in the year 2000, and we only have twenty years left. Darn!"

On the weekends, I hung out with some other friends, Pedro and Walter. We rode our bikes all over the neighborhood. We did pop a wheelies. I was able to do one for a block or two long. We also cruised down our city streets on roller skates. Most roller skates had a rubber brake on the front. Mine didn't, and the wheels on my skates were made out of metal. They were very cool and sleek. I skated everywhere with them, racing up and down hills, onto curbs, and over sidewalks.

There was a monster hill nearby. I was deathly afraid of it. But I knew I had to conquer it. So one day, I struck up the nerve to attempt it. I stood at the top of this behemoth, ready to plunge into the abyss. I took a deep breath, and with my trembling knees, I took a leap of faith. "Wee!" I shouted as I flew down the hill at top speed. My metal wheels made a loud screeching sound as flames and sparks shot out from underneath them as they made contact with the hard pavement. I repeated this stunt every day like clockwork. After performing this feat of bravery, I was inclined to touch the wheels of my roller skates. I touched them with my hands. And not surprisingly, they were scorching red hot. Eventually, my skates wore out, and the wheels popped off as I was whizzing down the hill one afternoon. Luckily, I wasn't seriously hurt, but my skates were totally ruined. Fun on the run. Yup!

60. West Side Story, 1980

The *West Side Story* is a spectacular movie, a modern Romeo-and-Juliet story. It was set in the streets of New York City. This film taught me two things: romance and racism. The Jerome Robbin's dance choreography was top-notch and unparalleled. The movie became an instant classic. It starred Natalie Wood, who portrayed Maria.

Maria was a young Puerto Rican girl. She fell in love with a young man named Tony. Tony and Maria first met at a high school dance. Tony was a member of the Jets. The Jets were mostly an Italian and Irish neighborhood gang. The gang was led by Tony's best friend, Riff. Maria's brother Bernardo was the leader of the Sharks, a local

Puerto Rican gang. Bernardo's right-hand man was Chino. Chino was very fond of Maria, but she absolutely had no interest in him.

I was ten years old when I first saw this movie. I had a big crush on Natalie Wood. She was very elegant and beautiful, the epitome of a true lady. I loved the movie. I felt it portrayed Puerto Ricans in a fair light. Bernardo was tough but had class and style. He was debonair and a great dresser. He was also very well spoken, a great leader, and showed great restraint. I wanted to be just like him. The movie showed both sides of the fence. It showed that both gangs were youths who truly cared about their family and friends. The fight scenes were great, and the musical score was incredible. The fight scenes had a martial arts flavor to them. The movie has award-winning performances throughout the film. Rita Moreno, a Puerto Rican actress, played Anita in the film. Throughout her illustrious career, she has won an Emmy, Tony, Grammy, and an Oscar. This is a must watch film! Yup.

61. Talent Show, 1981

The year was 1981. I lived in Jersey City, on Duncan Hill Avenue. I was attending PS 17. I was in the fifth grade. My brother was in the eighth grade. On one sunny afternoon, our school held a talent show for all the local kids. I was the school limbo champion. I was very flexible and had a very good sense of balance. Calypso music blasted from the large speakers as the kids competed in the limbo contest. I won the competition for a second year in a row. After the contest, it was time for the performances. There was a kid named Jimmy Baxley. He was a great gymnast. He did a variety of somersaults—back flips, front flips, semis, and arabians. He dazzled the audience. The crowd loved his performance and cheered wildly. There were other acrobats too. Reginald Moore and Barry Jefferson both did tumbling runs, a succession of rapid-fire back handsprings. Reggie did an impressive eleven flips in a row. Barry incredibly knocked out an astonishing seventeen backflips in one spot. Barry Jefferson had a small afro and reminded me of a young Michael Jackson from the Jackson 5. Barry always wore a pair of white Nike Cortez with a red stripe on the side.

I started hanging out with them every day after school. I wanted to learn and practice all I could from them. These kids reminded me of the *Five Deadly Venoms* from Channel 5. They were young but masterful with their acrobatic moves. With much practice, I was eventually able to do the same thing years later. My brother performed next with another group of acrobats, forming human pyramids. They did various dive rolls over all types of obstacles. It was really cool. My brother did dive rolls for weeks after, dive rolling over all the bushes in the neighborhood. After my brother's lively performance, my friend Shawn Whitehead performed a funky electro robot dance to the song "Trans-Europe Express."

Lastly, a tall, skinny Black gentleman wearing Coke bottle glasses with a fist pick sticking out of his afro was set to perform. He had long tube socks on worn with a pair of Chinese kung fu slippers. He also wore a white tank top with gym class blue bell-bottom shirts with a white stripe on its side. He looked like Roger from the 1970s *What's Happening!!* TV show. His dress attire was very common back then. The music started, and he spun around in circles, shuffling his feet quickly while bending at the knees. I found this performance very strange. He did similar movements like the Centipede character from the *Five Deadly Venoms* kung fu movie. Still, I thought it was rather odd. Finally, I asked my brother, "What the heck is he doing?"

Edward responded, "He's scrambling!"

"Huh?" I replied. This was my very first introduction into the world of breakdancing. I started breakdancing the year after. I used to robot, hustle, and salsa dance before. But this was a totally new and different experience for me. Yup.

62. Guardian Angels, Bronx, 1981

It was the summer of 1981. Mom decided to visit a friend named Betty. Betty was my uncle Paul's girlfriend. She lived in the Bronx. She had a son named Chucky. He was close to my age. They lived in an apartment on the corner of 190th Street and Morris Avenue. The building was in the Fordham Road section of the Bronx. I used to love going to his house. He had tons of toys. Mostly G. I. Joe and Star Wars action figures.

We lived in Jersey City during this time. Mom and I took the path train at Journal Square into Manhattan. We got off at Thirty-Third Street. We then transferred to the local subway. We took the uptown 4 Train to the Bronx. I remember the train whizzing out of the tunnel at 161st Street. I quickly peered out my left-side window and quickly took a glimpse of the live baseball game in Yankee Stadium. It was in the old stadium. You could see the field from the 4 Train elevated subway line. It was great!

We finally reached the Fordham Road station. We exited the train like we've done many times before. We walked down the long staircase to the street. There was a pizzeria right next to a small local movie theater named the Capri. Mom asked me, "Anthony, would you like some pizza?" I answered with a resounding "Yes!" She bought me two big cheesy, drippy, and super tasty in-your-face slices with pepperoni and a small Pepsi to wash it all down. I drank a lot of Pepsi back then. Coke was too harsh on my throat. I took my sweet time eating my mouthwatering slices of pizza. I wanted to savor the moment. Yum! They were so utterly delicious! I devoured my succulent food wholeheartedly. We then left the pizzeria to make our way toward Betty's apartment.

As we made our way to our destination we were suddenly approached by a knife-wielding maniac. He was very haggard and very dirty. Probably some homeless drug addict. A hobo. I was only ten years old, and I was absolutely terrified. I had a few lessons in karate, but I wasn't prepared for this. He lunged toward us with his blade shimmering in the light. He yelled, "Gimme some money!" Mom grabbed her purse and yanked my arm to turn and run. She screamed out loud.

Remember, this was 1981. There was a group of fed-up citizens so-called vigilantes patrolling the streets and subways of the big city. They wore red berets and red canvas jackets with an insignia of an angel's wings on the back—the Guardian Angels. The group was originally known as the Shaolin protectors / Magnificent 13. The organization was founded by Curtis Sliwa. Curtis Sliwa was a manager of a McDonald's restaurant on Fordham Road. He banded together with other locals who were sick and tired of the relentless amount of crime and lawlessness in the city. So he decided to make a difference. Cops were overworked and weren't always present when needed. Most citizens lived in fear behind closed doors. Turmoil took over the city. The Guardian Angels now has chapters all over the world.

Back to the story. So now, this man began attacking my mom with his knife. She screamed for someone to help. I felt so helpless. Several Guardian Angels were in the subway station. They heard my mother's panicked cries for help. About five or six of them came racing down the stairs. They reminded me of the heroes on the *Super Friends* cartoon, fighting for law and justice. Good versus evil. The Guardian Angels saw the villain and intercepted his attack. He lunged at them with his knife. They were very skilled in the martial arts and swiftly thwarted his weak attack. *Bang, bing, kaplunk, zoom!* Like a scene from the *Batman and Robin* TV show. They were agile and sharp in subduing the aggressor. All their movements were decisive and swift, calculating. They wore their red berets with colored beads dangling of the side and white T-shirts with the Guardian Angel logo crested on the front. Some had on kung fu pants and chinese slippers, just like Bruce lee. I totally admired them from then on forward. They were my real-life heroes.

My mom was very gracious and thankful. Most of the Guardian Angels were young, perhaps eighteen or nineteen, but nevertheless, they were amazing. Yup!

63. My Cousin David, 1981

I stood over my cousin David's house on some weekends. His mom was my mother's older sister. My mother had many brothers and sisters—my aunts Tenin, Teresa, Ana, Alicia, Rosa, Julia, Juanita, Matilda, Candita, and Aida and my uncles Isaiah, Mario, Manuel, Jose (Pepin), Pablo, Nacho, Enrique, etc. I had dozens of cousins as well. My aunt Ana had eight kids: Luis, Edwin, Tito, David, Ana Lou, Hillary, Nelly, and Maria.

David and I were the closest in age. We were only one year apart. We had many things in common. We both absolutely loved Captain Crunch breakfast cereal. It was loaded with sugar. It was totally bad for you. We ate tons of it. The sugar rush was incredible. After a few bowls, it was time to go out and play. We played in the park and in the streets and sometimes in the backyard. Occasionally, we'd jump on the fire escape and then hop onto roof. We also played tag, freeze tag, hide-and-seek, spin the bottle, man-hunt, and Skelzies (caps).

Skelzies, or Skelly, were played with bottle caps filled with tar or candle wax. Kids would show up with blastie caps, which were usually made with very large mayonnaise lids or jar lids. They would demolish all the other kids caps with an explosive thud.

We did many mischievous things, such as racking. Many under-privileged kids knew how to rack (steal) back in the days. There was a bodega (store) on the corner of David's house. He knew it very well. He had racked many items from the store throughout the years. The owners were Korean. The owners placed a small bell on the top side of the door. This was to alert them every time a customer entered the store. We had a plan though. My cousin went into the store first and spoke to the owner. He spoke very loudly to distract him, while the other naughty kids, including myself, snuck into the front of the shop. We were very careful not to ring the bell.

Someone actually held it and kept it from moving. That was when the rest of us juvenile delinquents made our move. We grabbed as many chips and drinks as possible. The chips and soda were the closest to the door. My cousin bought about five cents worth of penny candies. It was a great diversion. We executed our plan flawlessly. I guess we grew up watching too many World War II movies where the hero went behind enemy lines and infiltrated their ranks. David quickly exited the store. He joined our war party to share in the spoils of our completed mission—Dipsy Doodles, onion rings, cheese doodles, Wise potato chips, Doritos, Yoo-hoos, Maltas, Good-o-Colas, etc. We munched out and then played as usual. Yup.

64. Chase, Tia Ana, 1981

One afternoon, two dudes were waiting for me as I came out of school. They were both standing outside by the front entrance. Perhaps they wanted to invite me for a friendly cup of coffee. They weren't friends, that was for sure. I was not sure why they were out to get me. I was still attending PS 17 at the time. I lived right next door to the school, but I panicked and ran downhill further away from my house. Stupid move. These bastards gave chase. They chased me from Duncan Hill onto West Avenue. I made a right turn toward my Aunt Ana's home. I was in good shape and ran as fast as I could. Problem was, they were in shape too and didn't break a sweat. I ran and ran, trying my best to create some distance between us, which I did. *Once we get to my aunt Ana's house, I'll be safe. Besides, I have several older male cousins there who could help me out*, I thought optimistically.

After running for a few blocks at top speed, I made another quick right and turned onto a hill that led up to my aunt's block. I ran up to the front door and was ready to swoosh right in like I've always done before. It didn't work out that way though. The door was locked shut. "Damn!" I said to myself. I looked down the hill and saw these knuckleheads getting closer and closer. These dumb bastards must have done this before. They were very good at it. "Tia! Tia! Tia Ana!" I yelled out over and over again. My cries were in vain. Nobody was home that day. *Sheesh, lucky me*, I thought as I took off, and the two gentlemen pursued me. I dashed into a nearby park. As I entered the park, I stopped and turned to face my attackers and decided to stand my ground. I guess I felt very brave after watching the movie *The Warriors*, where a Coney Island gang got chased all over NYC and has to fight their way back home. The guys and I started fighting, and I got a few punches in, but they got the best of me.

Now I was pissed off and started crying hysterically. I yelled out at them, "Why you stupid motherfuckers!" I grabbed some large empty beer bottles that were lying about nearby and started tossing them at them. The bottles exploded on impact, making a loud thudding sound. They threw bottles back at me. It was a heated exchange.

At that point, I didn't give a shit. After the exchange, they took off. The craziest part of the whole scenario was that I didn't even know these bums. Yup!

65. The Smack, 1981

Ironically, my next fight—well, so-called fight—occurred in the same park where I had the beer-bottle clash. One morning, I let my mouth get the best of me. I was visiting my cousin David, and we decided to go for an early stroll in the park. David and I played on the seesaw, slide, and swings. There was a young girl close to our age playing in the park as well. She looked like the character Annie from the Broadway play. "Annie" had really curly red hair shaped like a small afro. David said, "That girl looks like the orphan Annie."

"Yes, she does look like her," I responded. My cousin went home to use the bathroom. I waited for him in the park. I started playing the fool and taunted the girl. I sang "The sun will come out tomorrow" over and over again. The young lady did her best to keep her composure as I belted out my horrendous version of the tune.

The girl finally got fed up and gave me a long hard stare, but I continued my foolish behavior and smiled back at her. She came off the slide and walked toward me to my surprise and, without uttering a single word, smacked the dickens out of me. I swear, I saw every star in the universe as they danced around my head. My face went totally numb. I could only hear the tone of a hung-up telephone line blaring in my ears. I was in total shock. The girl smiled at me and then walked away and exited the park. I also left the park and walked back to David's house in sheer disbelief. Yup.

66. Grandpa, Coney Island, Cyclone

My poor grandpa visited New York only once in his lifetime. My grandmother wanted him to visit his family. He was very reluctant but made the trip nevertheless. My grandfather was a farmer in his early life in Puerto Rico. The island's main crops for the most part were sugar and coffee. Grandpa had many offspring. Some of his sons and daughters moved from the island, relocating in New York. New York was very different from Puerto Rico. The city was very fast-paced, whereas the island's inhabitants were very relaxed and docile.

Grandpa reluctantly hopped on a plane and made the three-hour flight to New York. He brought his favorite panama hat with him. Grandpa reacquainted himself with his family as soon as he arrived. A few days later, the family decided to go to Coney Island for some summer fun. They snacked on some of the local delicacies, played carnival games, and decided to ride the legendary Cyclone. The Cyclone was a wooden roller coaster that was built in 1928. It was run down and unkept. My grandpa was tricked onto the ride. He had never ridden a coaster prior to this moment. Everyone said, "Get on! It's fun!"

"Are you sure?" he responded.

"Yeah, yeah, don't worry. Get on."

My grandpa, not aware of the dangerous and precarious nature of the ride, hopped on. He had his favorite hat on as he entered the ride. The ride took off slowly as it ascended to death-defying heights. I could only wonder what went through his mind during this time. In a moment, it whizzed down into the darkness below as all the riders screamed. Grandpa was in shock as his much-loved hat went flying into the unknown. The Cyclone screeched up and down and side to side as it bounced its riders all over the place. Grandpa held on for dear life. Finally, the ride came to a halt, as everyone gasped for air. My grandpa's shock now became anger as his face turned tomato red. He was irate and couldn't be consoled. He was so angry that he quickly booked a flight back to Puerto Rico to never return to the city again. Yup.

67. Odd Jobs, 1981

One early lesson our dad taught us was that "el mejor amigo de uno es un peso en el bosillo" translated meant "your best friend is a dollar in your pocket." I truly didn't understand this statement until I was much older. I've been homeless a few times. I've gone to bed hungry and didn't make enough money to pay my bills at certain times in my life. When I was down on my luck, very few people lent me a hand. One person I should mention would be my buddy Peter "Luli" Rodriguez. He let me stay with him when I hit the skids. Rock bottom. He was kind enough to share his home with me. His uncle Rafael (RIP) was very generous as well. He helped me receive free dental care when some of my teeth went bad. I sincerely want to thank these two gentlemen for their generosity toward me. I am eternally grateful.

Throughout our youth, my brother and I have always found different ways to make an honest buck. We mowed lawns, shoveled snow, packed bags at the supermarket, held yard sales, etc. We learned to hustle at an early age. Our parents supplied us with the basic things we needed, such as food, clothing, and shelter. My parents didn't approve of lazy, good-for-nothing kids. We were required to do our daily chores. We cooked, cleaned the house, did groceries, fixed things, etc. You name it, we did it. After doing our chores, our parents had us go out and make a few dollars.

Edward and I went to the local supermarket to pack bags. We both politely asked several customers, "Can I help you with your bags, ma'am or sir?" I was a few years younger than my brother, reminiscent of the *Leave It to Beaver* show. If I were the Beaver, then my brother was most definitely Wally, his older sibling. I had an innocent-looking face, a baby face. I was able to make quite a bit of money because of it. When I asked people if they needed help, they replied, "Aww, he's so cute." I had them in my pocket. Unfortunately, my brother struggled to make some change. At the end, we both counted our earnings. I was very proud that I had made a few bucks. My brother, on the other hand, wasn't too happy. He made paltry few cents. I loved my brother. I shared my profits with him. We bought a few slices of pizza and sodas. We also played video games.

Sometime later, my brother got a job working with our uncle Pepin. Uncle Pepin, or Tio Pepin as he was lovingly known, owned a used furniture store. He taught Edward how to refurbish and reupholster furniture. My brother was quite good and content at his newfound job. On some nights, I hung around the shop just to watch him work. Clip, clip, stitch, stitch, bam, bam. My brother was proficient with his work tools. This was our routine for a few weeks.

On one rainy evening, there was a break in the routine. There was some police activity across the street from the store. It was a chase scene right out of a movie. Several cops surrounded the building with their guns drawn. I still remembered their shiny silver pistols gleaming underneath the street lights. I was totally amazed. It reminded me of a TV episode of *S. W.A. T.* or *Starsky & Hutch*. Yup.

68. Bruce Lee Book, 1981

I lived on Duncan Hill Avenue for a short while in Jersey City, New Jersey. I had a close friend named Joseph. We were both eleven years old at the time. We basically did everything together, side by side and elbow to elbow. We played quite often with our toy army soldiers and Hot Wheels and Matchbox cars. On rainy days, we both played board games inside. We got along very well for the most part.

One day, my dad gave me a fine book to read as a gift. I loved reading. But this was no regular book. It was based on my real-life hero, the one and only martial arts legend Bruce Lee. I was a huge fanatic of all his electrifying films. This was the first book on him that I ever owned. I read the book day in and day out. I couldn't get enough of it. I was a happy camper. Joseph, on the contrary, didn't share the same feelings as I did. He couldn't care less about Bruce Lee.

One evening, Joseph and I came to a misunderstanding. We had an argument. I was at Joseph's house, and I decided to leave. I stormed out of the apartment and headed home. When I got home, I realized that I left my Bruce Lee book at Joseph's place. I panicked and quickly darted out the door and raced back toward his house. When I arrived back at Joseph's apartment, I noticed that my book was nowhere to be found. I asked Joseph, "Did you see my book?"

"No!" he adamantly replied.

From the corner of my eye, I could see something in the trash can. *Hmm, what could that be?* I thought. My eyes opened wider and wider as I stepped closer for a better look. What I saw next broke my heart. It was my dad's wonderful gift, shredded into bits and pieces.

I turned and looked back at Joseph, and he just lay on his bed and smiled at me with a devilish grin on his face.

Something overcame me, and I flew into a rage. I leaped across the bed like a leopard leaping onto his prey from a tall tree and landed right on top of Joseph. Without blinking an eye, I beat him into a pulp. He cried out loud, but it didn't matter now. It was time for justice to be served. I served it on a very hot plate. I was drenched in sweat from all the energy I exerted in the punishment of my foe. He continued lying there crying and whimpering like a lost, hungry kitten. He was covered in tears and bruises as he licked his wounds. I tried feeling remorse for him, but I just couldn't. After all, that dirty SOB destroyed my most beloved and treasured gift. *To hell with him!* I thought. His mother burst into the room and yelled at me and quickly escorted me out of the premises. Now it was I who walked home alone under the drizzling rain with a devilish smile on my face. Yup.

69. Whupping, Pacman, 1981

The year was 1981. I was eleven years old. My brother was thirteen. We lived on Duncan Hill Avenue in Jersey City, New Jersey. Our home was right next to PS 17, which we both attended. I was in the fifth grade. My brother was in the eighth grade. On the weekends, we hung out in the local game rooms. Video games were extremely popular back then. You could find them in all the mom-and-pop grocery shops.

We played all the latest games—Pacman, Galaxian, Robotron: 2084, Wizard of Wor, Tron, Donkey Kong, Moon Cresta, Tempest, Satan's Hollow, Kangaroo, Lady Bug, Berzerk, Galaga, Space Invaders, Defender, Asteroids, etc. If we weren't in the game room, then we were on the streets playing tag, freeze tag, stickball, hide-and-seek, cops and robbers, manhunt, Skelzies, spin the bottle, etc. We played outside till the sun set or when the street lights came on. That was the rule in most homes back then. If you broke the rule, then you were grounded. One night, our dad brought home a Pong video game unit. It was in black-and-white only. There were three games built in, which included Pong, Breakout, and Skeet. There was a plastic gun included with the unit. You needed it to play Skeet. We spent hours playing all three games. We loved them.

One Sunday, at about 3:00 p.m., Edward and I were sent to the supermarket by our parents. They sent us to buy some ingredients for dinner. We were also instructed to buy two small packs of cigarettes, Marlboros for my dad and Kools for Mom. Kids were allowed to purchase cigarettes back then. Today, the law has changed. The minimum age to purchase cigarettes is twenty-one years of age. Before we left the house, our parents gave us a twenty-dollar bill. They said, "You can have one dollar for each of you." Everything was very cheap in those days. The total change for everything was thirteen dollars.

We quickly headed for the game room. The game room was packed with kids. The sound from the video games bounced off the walls. Pacman was absolutely the most popular game at the time. There were rows and rows of quarters placed on top of the game, groups of kids waiting to play next. We set our quarters on top and joined in the frenzy. We had a field day not realizing how much money we had spent or how much time had passed by. As we left the game room, we took notice of how late it was. We realized that we had spent all the money—every single red cent. It was pitch-black dark outside, almost 10:00 p.m. We had to be back in ten minutes. *Damn!* I thought fearfully. We were in for it. An ass beating was eminent. I looked at my brother with trepidation. He returned the same look.

We slowly approached our house. I was scared out of mind. It felt like Halloween in June. Dinner was ruined on our behalf, and my parents were itching to smoke. Mom and Dad, for sure's sake, must've been heated. We rang the bell several times, but no one answered. We knocked really hard on the door, and yet again, no response. We started banging on the window, almost breaking it. A light came on in our house. I gasped in anticipation of what was to come. Finally, the door opened wide, and there stood a small non-threatening woman. She was concealing something behind her back. *What could it be?* I pondered in my thoughts. Mom was only 5 feet 3 inches tall, but tonight she was a giant among men. Standing by the doorway, she appeared to be eight feet tall. A sasquatch! She burned a hole right through us as she looked down on Edward and me from the porch. She snarled like a sabretooth tiger on the prowl. I could vaguely see that she had a leather belt tightly clenched around her hand. It was one of the skinny types that burned deep into the flesh. Dad preferred the thick leather variety, which felt like punches when it hit you.

Edward and I tried explaining to Mom our reasons for coming home at the time that we did. We came up with all sorts of excuses as to why we were so late. Mom wasn't having any of it. She ardently blocked the doorway like a linebacker from the New York Giants as she kept us from entering. I tried making a run for it and squeezing my way between her and the doorway. I didn't make it. *Thump! Whack!* She caught me in the middle of my back. The crack of that belt really sizzled. She hit me three or four times with a thud. She was like Zorro with a blade. My brother got plenty of love too. We both cried and shrieked like frightened mice. We darted to our rooms to lick our fresh wounds. No dinner that night. Lesson learned. Dad watched with a smile. Yup!

70. Eric Boyd, 1981

Growing up was very difficult. I was rather shy around people that I didn't know well. I only opened up to my relatives or close friends. Our family was constantly packing up and moving from one place to another. It was very unsettling for me. I felt really nervous and anxious every time I attended a new school. And I tried my very best to fit in and make new friends. My palms got sweaty as I always felt all eyes glaring on me. "Who's the new kid?" some students asked. For some reason the vultures (bullies) found me on their radar. *Those rotten bastards!* I thought. It's amusing now, but it was a very harrowing experience back then.

One bully in particular was Eric Boyd. He was much taller than me. I was in the fifth grade. We both attended PS 17 in Jersey City. He was left back twice. This shmuck had it in for me. He insulted me every day and eyeballed me as he tried his best to degrade me.

Eric was a true asshole in every sense of the word. I was living a nightmare! (Kids getting bullied in school was a very serious problem. Back in the days, you were pretty much on your own, unlike today where most school officials intervene on the victim's behalf. It was survival of the fittest.) So day after day, I had to deal with the constant taunting and bullshit from this idiot. I was reaching a boiling point.

That moment came on the school stairwell. Eric was behind me and kept slapping my legs as we walked up the stairs. I told him to stop. But being the piece of crap that he was, he decided to continue irritating me. I instinctively placed a hard back kick square on his face. He was livid and very angrily shouted, "I'll get you after school!" Eric Boyd had revenge on his mind. "Shit!" I whispered. I was done for. I practiced a bit of karate, but nothing serious. I dibble dabbled in it. I wish I had been more serious about training up to this point. Actually, it was no fault of my own; my parents always made the decisions to pack and move. Unfortunately, I never had the chance to settle down and get serious about anything.

I was in a dire situation, but I must admit I felt really good about kicking him in the head, even though I knew a beating was coming my way. My brother used to attend PS 17 but graduated and then started attending PS 11 across town. My brother Edward was street savvy, tough, a real good fighter. I, on the other hand, loved the Bee Gees, *West Side Story,* Kenny Rogers, Barry Manilow, etc. I was the romanticist. Love was on my mind, not violence; but there was no escaping the doom that awaited me. My brother always backed me up, but this time, I was on my own.

It was 3:00 p.m. The bell rang for dismissal. I planned my escape. I tried exiting through a side door, hoping that the demon child wouldn't see me. I wondered, "Maybe he's still in the building?" As I turned the corner, my heart sank. I felt a lump in my throat. Eric Boyd was waiting like he promised. The SOB was punctual. On time. "Damn!" I whispered. Pretending not to see him, I made my way up a hill, trying to hide among the crowd leaving the school. Like a wolf sniffing out his prey, he trailed close behind me. I saw my friend Alan and struck up a conversation. Eric Boyd yelled out my name.

A large mob of kids gathered behind us in anticipation of a fight. My friend asked, "Don't you know karate?"

"Not really," I responded.

A look of concern crossed his face. I started walking faster and faster, trying to avoid the overzealous mob. I should've run away, but my pride didn't allow me to. We crossed the avenue. We were a few blocks from the school now. I was in open territory. I didn't want to fight Eric. Seeing me trying to get away gave him more energy for his attack.

I had on Buster Brown shoes with high water pants and a sweater. I heard the sound of quick shuffling footsteps behind me reminiscent of a horror film. Suddenly, Eric leaped into the air. I felt his massive foot make impact with the small of my back. Wham! I flew up in the air and flipped forward, landing on my hands and knees several feet from where I was standing. I was totally humiliated and crushed. My hands and knees were bloodied and scraped. I cried, not because of the pain I felt. I cried because I felt hopeless, powerless. My clothes were ripped and ruined. I went home with my tail in between my legs. My parents were furious. "Why didn't you pick up a stick?" they asked.

"None were available, thank you very much!" I chirped in anger.

The next morning, I left the house with a large kitchen knife, the biggest one I could find and the same one that Michael Myers used in the movie *Halloween. Time for some payback!* I thought. "That motherfucker, he's dead!" I said pissed off as I made my way to school. "How dare he?" As I made my usual route, I noticed Eric Boyd and a gang of his friends waiting on the other block. Those asswipes were hiding in the bushes, waiting to ambush me. "Motherfuckers!" I said, holding my knife trembling. Payback was on my mind. But there were too many of them, about five or six of them. I quietly backtracked my steps and went back home. My parents had had enough. They took me to school that morning, and they sternly spoke to the principal. Eric and I faced each other in the office. He was heavily reprimanded and was suspended. I was free of this demon. Thank God! Yup.

71. Lonely Walks to Music, 1981

My young life was definitely not a stroll in the park. Our dysfunctional family was always in a state of turmoil. I loved my parents, but their antics and constant bickering created a very unstable home for my brother and me. They truly cared about us; unfortunately, they were too busy going at each other's throats. I had to fill the gaps. My brother was doing his own thing, hanging out with his friends and girlfriends, so I had to find my own way. Music was a good escape for me. I spent countless hours listening to the great music of the 1970s and early 1980s—artists that included but not limited to the Bee Gees, Barry Manilow, the Eagles, Diana Ross, Michael Jackson, Andy Gibb, Abba, Donna Summer, Jefferson Starship, Kenny Rogers, Lionel Richie, Frankie Valli, etc. There were so many romantic and beautiful songs I loved to sing such as "Magic," "Lady," "What a Night," "How Deep Is Your Love," "Endless Love," and "Miracles." I remember walking the city streets at night and looking up at the stars in the sky while singing these classics. I memorized all the lyrics.

I was truly a loner and had only a handful of friends, mostly because we were always moving. Constantly adapting to my new environments became a way of life for me. Someone gave our family an organ as a gift. I wrote my first song on it called "Unbelievable." I sang it every day to my heart's delight. Dancing was also a great hobby for me too. Disco, salsa, rock, hustle, and later on, electric boogie and breakdancing (B-boying) filled my days. A lot of youngsters escaped from their everyday problems in this manner back then. I was always fighting with bullies, so eventually, I heavily indulged myself into the martial arts. Training day in and day out helped stabilize my feelings and personal life. Tormented from my parents constantly lashing out at each other, the martial arts really helped to center me. I had no control over my surroundings, but I had the power over my inner self, the choice to be who I wanted and to live how I felt was right.

Throughout the years, it has been an uphill battle. I trusted few people and still do. My personal relationships were not perfect, but I guess none are. I've gone through some rough patches, some not-so-happy life experiences. With time, I learned about the love of God, self-love, and the love of community. Most importantly, I learned that people will let you down, which is a fact you cannot change, but pick yourself up, dust yourself off, wipe your tears, and keep moving forward. Yup!

72. Saturday Kung Fu, TV PIXX, King Kong vs. Godzilla, 1981

New York's metro area's WNEW channel 5 and WPIX's channel 11 were rivals in the '70s and '80s. Both channels always competed for viewership. WOR channel 9 as well. The three rivals weren't major networks such as ABC, NBC, or CBS, but they packed a punch. They all played classic cartoons the likes of *Woody Woodpecker*, *Looney Tunes*, *The Jetsons*, *Tom and Jerry*, etc., also TV reruns *The Twilight Zone*, *The Honeymooners*, *Star Trek*, etc. Channel 11 was also known for TV PIXX. TV PIXX was an after-school program that highlighted video games. Kids called the station and shouted "Pixx, Pixx, Pixx" over the phone. Whoever scored the highest points during the game won a prize.

WPIX also ran the Chiller series for several years. Chiller showcased classic horror films. Channel 9 bounced back with the Fright Night series. Channel 5 debuted kung fu chop-socky classics at 3:00 p.m. every Saturday. The first two martial arts movies that aired were *Master Killer*, a.k.a. *The 36th Chamber of Shaolin*, and *Bruce Lee: His Last Days, His Last Nights*. WNEW channel 5 also ran the *Big Apple* movie at 6:00 p.m. every Sunday, which showcased several Bruce Lee films. Channel 11 got into the mix by playing a kung fu double feature. This type of television programming ran for several years throughout the '70s and '80s. *King Kong, Godzilla, Mighty Joe Young*, and other classic flicks were also part of the lineup. Turning into the '90s, the programs disappeared and were mostly replaced with infomercials. Yup.

73. Bobby and Maria, 1981

I had several cousins living in Jersey City in 1981. Bobby and Maria were some of the most memorable ones. They had two children named Arland and Tamara. Arland was close to my age. Tamara was much younger. Arland and I played with action figures and miniature cars mostly outside, and Tamara played in her room with her dolls. Bobby and Maria were supercool. Maria was my first cousin and daughter of my oldest aunt, Ana. She was married to Bobby. Bobby always sported a short afro, reminiscent of the artist Bob Ross. Maria was very beautiful and elegant like the leading character Maria from the film *West Side Story*. Our family spent a lot of time at their house. Our parents played cards while the kids played outside. Occasionally, we'd cross the street to play in a local area playground called Liberty State Park. The kids ran around the park while our parents chatted up a storm. After running around for several hours, we'd get winded and hungry. Our parents served up some homemade sandwiches or ordered a pizza pie. We all sat down and chomped away.

In the evening, we played Atari with Bobby. It was the first colorized home video game I had ever seen up to that point. Our Pong game was black-and-white and seemed very ordinary in comparison. The Atari unit also had cartridges for different games. I thought it was the most amazing thing ever. Bobby had Air Sea Battle and Combat. My dad purchased a copy for my brother and I later on. After playing for several hours, it was time for dinner and then a movie. Maria and Mom cooked together. Maria was a great cook. She made a very good carne guisada. After a great meal, we were now ready for a great film. WHT was the most popular cable service at the time. We watched several movies such as *The Island* and *Dressed to Kill* which starred Angie Dickinson from the *Police Woman* TV series. Our parents covered our eyes anytime a movie showed an inappropriate scene for youngsters. We always tried to sneak a peek. There was also the steamy and raunchy *Nightcap* programming, which was for adults only. During the early hours of the day, Arland and I watched several martial arts movies such as *Enter the Ninja* and *Exit the Dragon, Enter the Tiger*. It was good times with our families. Yup!

74. Tito and Millie, 1981

My cousin Tito was several years older than me. He was super-cool and always treated me with kindness. He was Maria's brother. His wife's name was Millie. Every time our family came by for a visit, Millie would make a batch of coffee and served them with pastries that I so happily devoured. Tito was very street savvy. He always called me B, which was short for Bially. He always rocked the coolest kicks (sneakers) such as flat suede Pumas, PRO-Keds, and the classic Converse All Stars. We spent quite a bit of time at his house. Edward and I played the board game Connect 4 for many hours in his kitchen. Tito always carried a boom box and always blasted New York radio station 92 KTU with the legendary host Paco. Paco was a radio personality who had a very deep, booming voice. He sounded like the character Darth Vader from the *Star Wars* films. Rap music was becoming extremely popular on the air waves during this time, and disco was basically dead for most radio aficionados at this point. One evening, our family celebrated Tito's birthday at a local nightclub. It was in downtown Jersey City. An early '80s rap group performed that evening. I can't recall which group hit the stage that night, but what I do remember is them chanting "Say ho, Say Al" and dazzling the audience.

Tito had a good friend named Nano. Nano dressed in the trendiest fashions and always rocked the latest sneakers. He also wore his hair in a short buzz cut while Tito sported a sleek short afro. My brother and I would hang out with Tito in Nano's basement. Nano had a small gym setup. He had a weightlifting bench with several barbells and dumbbells. The weighted plates were the old plastic sand-filled type. We spent several hours exercising in the dusty, spider web–filled basement. Even though I was only eleven years old at the time, my cousin Tito always treated me with respect and kindness and did his best to educate me on things he felt I should know. He was very caring and took his time to make me feel like I mattered in the great scheme of things. Unfortunately, he was stabbed to death several years later, trying to protect his mom from some would-be robbers. RIP, my cool cousin Tito. Yup!

75. Motivations, 1982

I had several motivations for training in the martial arts. The first and foremost was Bruce Lee. His incredible movies and TV show *The Green Hornet* inspired the hell out of many generations. He was the epitome of fitness. There were others before Lee in terms of fitness. Steeve Reeves from the *Hercules* movies came to mind, Johnny Weissmuller from the *Tarzan* movies, and George Reeves from the *Superman* TV show as well. But none of them moved like Bruce Lee. Bruce Lee was extremely fast with cat-like reflexes, and those kicks were lightning. His moves and dazzling display of skill and will mesmerized fans.

Another major inspiration of mine was Sylvester Stallone in the *Rocky* movie. The training sequences were outstanding and put fire in my heart. It also had a great soundtrack. The running scene where he ran through the streets of Philadelphia was epic. *Star Wars* made me want to be a Jedi. Luke Skywalker was awesome. "Use the force"— totally adrenaline-driven action. I loved it. The musical soundtrack was out of this world.

My family watched all the championship boxing matches. We sat in front of the TV and watched greats such as Muhammad Ali, Sugar Ray Leonard, Salvador Sánchez, Roberto Durán, Thomas Hearns, Wilfred Benítez, Larry Holmes, Earnie Shavers, Alexis Argüello, Marvin Hagler, Aaron Pryor, Ray Mancini, Wilfredo Gómez, etc. The gladiators, the fighting spirit, the never-give-up attitude—I learned by watching those warriors ply their craft. Mom always cooked up some delicious food as we witnessed some historic fights.

Wrestling also played a huge role in my motivation. I grew up watching the legends of the small screen—Bob Backlund, Jimmy "Superfly" Snuka, Ivan Putski, Andre the Giant, Randy "Macho Man" Savage, Ken Patera, Rocky Johnson, Hulk Hogan, Tito Santana, etc. The goliaths of the squared jungle and pure physical specimens of wrath, they were chiseled and strong with super Herculean abilities. Athletic and charismatic strongmen always ready to tangle at a moment's notice. Daredevils who leaped, jumped, and skyrocketed off the top ropes for our amusement.

Etched deep into my memory was Terry Fox. He was a victim of cancer. One of his legs was amputated. Amazingly enough, he mustered up the will to run across Canada and the USA with the whole world glued to their TV sets, watching daily in support. Sadly, he succumbed to the disease. A real hero. My hero.

A female hero of mine was a young Romanian gymnast by the name of Nadia Comăneci, who took the entire gymnastics world by storm by scoring the first perfect 10 in the Olympics. I was absolutely intrigued by this skinny, demure young lady who became one of the all-time greatest athletes to ever compete in the Olympic games. Astounding. Yup.

76. Restaurant Business with Family Friend Naco, 1982

Dad had an old friend named Naco who lived in Bridgeport, Connecticut. Naco owned a small diner and wanted to bring Dad in as a business partner, so my parents decided to pack up and move to Bridgeport in 1982. We moved into a studio attic apartment on Arctic Street. It was cozy with two small rooms and a kitchenette but was very comfortable. There was a small porch in the back of the studio. I spent many nights gazing at the stars from that viewpoint. One afternoon, a thunderstorm rolled into the neighborhood. Edward and Mom were standing on the porch. I was too scared to join them, so I just watched the storm from behind the screen door. They both chided me and said, "Don't be afraid. Come outside, it's beautiful."

I replied, "No, no, no, the lightning."

They both laughed when suddenly—*boom!* A huge lightning bolt crackled and ripped across the sky barely reaching into the porch. Edward and Mom panicked as they shuffled their feet, trying to scramble away from the lightning bolt. They both smashed through the screen door like Tom and Jerry as I was overcome by laughter. Ha ha.

Over the next several weeks, my parents ran the diner without a hitch, cooking and cleaning day in and day out as the customers rolled in. They served fried eggs and bacon for breakfast and burgers and fries for lunch. For dinner, rice and beans with fried pork chops, steak, or chicken was served. Beef stew was also on the menu. I could still remember the sizzle and smell of the food grilling on the stove. Coffee was a main staple at the diner. The restaurant business didn't last long however. I guess the bump and grind caught up with my parents. They weren't used to the constant daily hustle and, eventually, burned out. Due to financial hardship, my dad was forced to find work elsewhere. He found a very good job doing auto body work on trucks in Milford. It was near the Sikorsky helicopter airport. Mom used to drive her Vega to pick him up from work every day at 5:00 p.m. I always accompanied her on the short drives with my dog Chegui in hand. He was a very cute Chihuahua. Dad was good working with his hands and did well at his job for a while.

One afternoon, I was sitting home watching the news when I heard that a tractor trailer truck had crashed on the Connecticut State freeway. It seemed that the driver fell asleep at that wheel and slammed his massive 18-wheeler truck into unsuspecting drivers lined up at a toll. There was a large explosion. There were many fatalities. My dad's auto body shop was assigned to recover the damaged vehicles, including the truck. The workers saw limbs and body flesh strewn about the crash location. It was horrendous sight.

A few months later, Dad started doing auto body work from the backyard of our home. He did a lot of side jobs. He always tried to get Edward and me to take an interest in it. We learned how to change oil, fix flats, rebuild carburetors, and repair dents on cars. We helped him out whenever we could, but in all honesty, we were totally uninterested in his profession. Later on in life, some of the skills we learned from him came in handy when we had cars of our own. Thanks, Dad. Yup.

77. The Chase, Brother, Bikes, 1982

Being the new kid on the block wasn't so easy. I left Eric Boyd, the demon child, way back in the slums of New Jersey. It was now time for a fresh start in Bridgeport. Little did I know that shadows could be found in all forms of light. Regardless, I was very happy in my newfound home. We relocated into a nice neighborhood, or so it seemed. We moved into a small studio attic apartment. It was very nice with a small bedroom and kitchenette. We also had free HBO—well, actually, it was an illegal hotbox. You'd pay some local street urchins ten bucks, and they would climb the telephone poles and hook you up. Edward and I spent countless hours watching movies such as the following: *Wolfen*; *Caveman*; *Young Frankenstein*; *Scanners*; *History of the World, Part 1*; *Porky's*; *The Last American Virgin*; *Search and Destroy*; *The Challenge*; *The Earthling*; *Ghost Story*; *Trading Places*; *Arthur*; *American Werewolf in London*; *Taps*; *Poltergeist*; etc. We also watched plenty of stand-up comedy with Eddie Murphy, Richard Pryor, and George Carlin, also the comedy skits *of Not Necessarily the News* and *Fraggle Rock*. Our family watched all the HBO boxing fights with stars like Sugar Ray Leonard, Alexis Argüello, Tommy Hearns, Larry Holmes, Marvin Hagler, Wilfred Benítez, and Roberto Durán just to name a few.

When Edward and I weren't watching TV, then we were out and about exploring our new stomping grounds. We spent a lot of time in the corner grocery store playing video games. My brother loved Dig Dug, Donkey Kong, and Moon Cresta. I enjoyed Kangaroo, Galaxian, and Lady Bug. Mom bought Edward and me a new wardrobe to start out the new school year. We were very poor, but nevertheless, she always found a way to buy clothes for us. She understood the importance of a good education and did her very best to make us feel comfortable on our first day of school. I started attending Beardsley Elementary School in Bridgeport. I was in the sixth grade. Beardsley Elementary was a nice school. The teachers were very attentive to the students' needs. Edward, on the other hand, was attending Harding High School.

My first day at Beardsley started out well. I was assigned a classroom seat and met all my new classmates. We all introduced ourselves to one another and then proceeded to our lessons. I was having a great time in my new school. The lunch bell rang as all the kids lined up for some nourishment. I ate my tasty, hot lunch and finished it off with a cool, refreshing chocolate milk. I was very quiet and sat for a while and observed my surroundings. The next few days went off without a hitch. I made a few acquaintances here and there. Eventually, I once again found myself in the cafeteria during lunchtime enjoying a delectable meal. All the kids had their faces buried deep in their plates, enjoying a smorgasbord of delights. From the corner of my eye, I could see a face in the crowd with their eyes fixated on me. It was a friendly young girl named Yvette. She was in my class and helped me settle into my new school. She explained the school routines and made me feel at home. Unbeknown to me, a pack of wolves were watching nearby. They had blood on their minds. Their leader had a massive crush on Yvette and saw me as an intrusion. His name was Louie. He was a clumsy-looking big kid who towered over me in height. That afternoon, for some reason, he decided to sit at my table. He fixed his vision on me and began making derogatory comments, jokes so to speak. I, in self-defense, snapped back. All the kids on the table cracked up in laughter except for my new friend Louie. He looked at me with fire-red eyes and said, "I'll get you after school!" Where have I heard those words before. *Damn, not again!* I thought.

The school bell rang for dismissal. I quickly exited the building through the back door. I worked my way around to the playground and climbed through a hole in the fence, almost scratching my back off in the process. I ran across the street and saw my buddies waiting for me on the other intersection. King Louie and his men, surprised to see me, gave chase, but it was too late, for I was too far gone. When I got home, I told my brother what had happened. He said, "Don't worry!"

I said, "Are you sure?"

"Yeah, I'll pick you up tomorrow after school with all my home-boys!" he responded.

I was like "Oh yeah, thanks, bro!"

The next day, I went to school feeling reassured that my brother and his hulking football player friends from high school had my back. That day in the lunchroom, I was defiant as ever. King Louie and his rejects of the suburbs tried insulting me once again, but I snapped back ever so confidently and reduced them all to shreds with my juvenile words of wisdom. I stirred up the hot soup of rebellion, and now these fools were surely out to get revenge.

The school bell rang, and once again, I tried using the same modus operandi. I hastily exited through the back door and with a big confident smirk on my face. I worked my way around to the front of the building. I was feeling elated and floated above the clouds with every step that I took. Once I turned the corner, I was sure to see my brother and the Avengers waiting to safely escort me home. My mouth dropped agape when I came to the clear realization that my brother forgot to set his watch. *Holy shit!* I thought. Louie was on the corner waiting for me. I hastily ran to the backyard of the school to escape. It wasn't to be for King Louie had placed some of his goons by the playground, blocking off the opening in the fence. I zigzagged my way around the school and ran down another block. The goon squad were hot on my tracks. I ran like my life depended on it. *Where in the hell is my brother Edward?* I pondered as I scurried my way home. The bad boys were close on my tail. They started gaining ground as my legs numbed up from the chase. I was about to get caught up in the fly trap when, out of nowhere, a bunch of dudes on bikes came whizzing down the street. They were on ten-speed bikes. It was the calvary! My brother came through for me. Thank God! They jumped off their bikes and pummeled and body slammed King Louie and his goons. They gave them a royal-ass beating. No one messed with me at school after that. Heck, no one even looked in my direction.

For the next few days, I looked out for my brother's needs. I made him sandwiches, poured his cereal, and did his house chores. From then on, my brother was the king. Thank you, bro. Yup!

78. The Brick, Ruben, Schoolyard, 1982

My brother had a close friend named Ruben. They were about the same age. His nickname was Ronald McDonald because of his oversized lips. Ruben was a neighborhood hoodlum. He always wore flat-bottomed Pumas with fat laces. He used to hang out with my brother at a park near my home. Ruben was cool for the most part, but one afternoon, he got the itch to crack jokes. I was good at cracking jokes myself. I wasn't in a good mood that day and really had no interest in any games of any sort. Ruben was being a ball buster and started teasing me. I told him to stop. I was very quiet, but my temperature was rising. I was ready to erupt. My brother saw that I was about to snap and told Ruben, "Yo, chill out. He's getting mad!" Ruben kept on and on. That was it; I reached my breaking point. I totally snapped. I saw a large red brick on the side of the schoolyard and picked it up. Ruben said, "Yo, get your little brother!"

Edwin said, "Didn't I say to stop messing with him!"

I chased Ruben all around the school yard with a brick in my hand with the intent of cracking him across the skull. "Argh!" I yelled out. I chased him for a few minutes.

Ruben was winded and said, "Your brother is nuts!" My brother laughed. Ruben never bothered me again. Yup.

79. Arcade, Spanky's, the Wizard, Playland, '80s

Video games were the talk of the town in the 1980s. There were two local arcades near my home. One was called Spanky's, and the other was called the Wizard. Spanky's was much larger than the Wizard and had tons of games that stretched out for row after row. Spanky's had all the latest games, which included Dragon's Liar, a state-of-the-art cartoon game. Spanky's offered five tokens for one dollar, whereas the Wizard offered eight tokens for the same. Most games only cost one token to play. My brother and I spent countless hours playing the latest games as well as the classics. The arcades were always full of kids trying their best to beat the videos. Some pinball machines were also available for those who liked the older form of entertainment. We usually spent our Friday evenings enjoying the spectacle of lights and colors that emanated from all the screens across the arcade. The sounds were mesmerizing. It was a simple and joyous time for us.

Later on, I spent time playing video games at Playland located at Times Square, NYC. I frequented this spot quite often, sometimes alone or with friends. It was a sleazy joint with scoundrels hiding in the shadows. You always had to look over your shoulder and keep a sharp eye and lookout for pickpockets. They were everywhere. Regardless, they had all the coolest games, so I spent some cash at the joint.

Sadly, today, most of the arcades are gone. Technology has made it easier for gamers to engage in their pastime and play video games from their homes. Gaming units such as Nintendo, PlayStation, and Xbox have sold billions of dollars in merchandise. The fact was videos games were here to stay. I'm glad I was able to experience the golden era of arcades, which will always have a place in my heart. Yup.

80. Snowball, Teacher, Police, Mom, 1982

In the winter, especially after a large snowfall, kids loved going out and playing in the snow, making snowmen, throwing snowballs, sledding down hills, building igloos, and forming snow angels. I also enjoyed partaking in these activities. Unfortunately, I got into serious trouble because of it. One day, while I was in school, it started snowing very heavily. I was in the sixth grade. The principal decided to let the students dismiss from school a bit earlier. All the kids were happy to hear the good news. I started walking home with my friend Jeffrey. We always hung out together and were basically sidekicks. As we made our way home, we caught a glimpse of a couple of yellow school buses at an intersection. The kids on the buses called us names and gave us the finger. I said, "What, how dare you!" Jeffrey and I, looking to get some quick payback, rolled up some snow and threw them at the buses. The snowballs made a loud whizzing sound as they flew with a menace toward their targets. The snowballs hit their mark with a thud. The kids cursed us out even more. One of them even mooned (bared his bottom at) us. We loved it. We continued bombarding the buses with snowballs as they made a wide turn at the intersection. At that instance, a car pulled up behind the bus. The car had its windows pulled down, and one of our snowballs accidently went in. It struck the driver in the face as he pressed down on his brakes, making an ear-piercing screeching sound. The driver, red faced with anger, quickly looked in our direction. We hastily ducked behind some bushes, but it was too late. He yelled out our names, "Anthony and Jeffrey, get back to the school now!" It was our social studies teacher. He looked like the character from *Mr. Rogers' Neighborhood* but wasn't so pleasant.

I knew I was in for it. "Oh god, I'm in trouble!" I told Jeffrey. He looked worried too. We both walked back to our school with our heads down very slowly, retracing our footprints in the snow. We were brought into the office. A police cruiser pulled up to the school, and a tall officer handcuffed both of us as we were put into the vehicle. My eyes welled up with tears at this juncture. He drove us downtown to the local police precinct. I started crying hysterically while seated in the booking room. Jeffrey got nervous and teary-eyed when he saw me breakdown. I wasn't scared of the cops; I was terrified of how my parents would react. We were just two kids playing with snowballs, and after all, it was an accident, and we apologized. But now we were being treated like juvenile delinquents. The cops saw that I felt remorse. A few minutes later, Mom and Dad entered the precinct. The officer-in-charge explained to my parents what had occurred. Mom looked down at me, sitting on the bench while I was drenched in tears, and asked, "Eso es verdad?" (Is that true?) I slowly looked up at her crying and said "Yes." She smacked me real hard right in front of everyone. There were many cops and detectives in the room, but they just kept about their business. Parents had more rein on how they disciplined their children back then. It was a tough day for me. Jeffrey and I never hung out together after that miserable experience. Damn snowballs! Yup!

81. Bruce Lee Chucks, 1982

In 1982, our family packed up and moved from Jersey City, New Jersey, to Bridgeport, Connecticut. My first goal was to reestablish my martial arts training. I quickly scrambled to make some new friends. I made friends with a local Puerto Rican family. They were Edwin, Eggy, and Maggie Quiniones. They were from a very tight-knit family. Later on, I made friends with some Dominican brothers named Gustavo, Raul, and Vladimir.

They were all really cool. We all hung out together. We played street games and cracked jokes. We also watched kung fu movies and WWF wrestling on TV. We spent a huge amount of time together. One thing we all had in common was the love for Bruce Lee. Bruce Lee was masterful with his dazzling display of nunchakus in his films. Because of his influence and my creativity at the time, I started making chucks from old brooms and mops I found on the street. I also used old dog chains to bond the sticks together.

It became a lucrative business—well, at least for a twelve-year-old kid. My chucks went for a $1.50 a pair. They sold like hotcakes. I sold about twenty pairs a week, all colors including red, black, yellow, green, silver, blue, etc. I used some of my father's duct tape, which he kept around the house, to decorate them. Once I had enough money saved, I started to invest in my business and bought supplies. I did very well for a bit. All the local kids and hooligans from the neighborhood were now equipped with a replica Bruce Lee pair of head knockers. Nunchakus! Waya!

I wanted to share some of my earnings with my friends. I always went to the local bodega (grocery store) and bought a few bags of five-cent Icees, about two or three dollars' worth. It was scorching hot outside in the summer. The kids were running around all day. They played all types of games and ended up sweaty, thirsty, and exhausted. I decided to share my Icees with my all friends. A steady rush of children swarmed around me as I began tossing Icees in every direction. It was a madhouse! They were like savages in the deep jungles of no man's land! Yup!

82. Senpai Rob, 1982

Sometimes, local kids hung out at the library or the community center. A sweet old lady who was very kind with us ran the community center. She brought in her nephew who was an accomplished karate instructor to teach self-defense. The kids referred to him as Senpai Rob.

Senpai Rob was a young Black man. He was about twenty years old. He had braids in his hair. He wore a karate uniform that was rather worn-out. I guess it showed that he had some experience. He was a brown belt, one of those old-school, tough, and hard-core busted-up-knuckle brown belts. He was a student of a very well-known local karate instructor named Matty Melisi. Matty Melisi had a martial art show that aired on a local TV station.

My friends Edwin, Eggy, Gustavo, Vladimir, Raul, and I all joined the class. I had prior martial arts experience. But I was not technically proficient up to this point. I was ecstatic to start training again. Oh, man, he really tortured us. He made us do a gazillion knuckle pushups on the hard marble floor. We all shook. Our arms trembled nonstop as the perspiration poured from our brows. The sweat danced around our heads. He barked commands like a prison warden. He was relentless. We suffered. Block, kick, strike, bend, stretch, pushups, sit ups, mountain climbers, jumping jacks, squats, etc.—it was very grueling. I loved it. Unfortunately, the classes ended after a few weeks. Now, I was in limbo again. Argh!

Our training was just like the kung fu movies where the pupil gets tortured by the master. Some of these movies with excruciating training sequences include but are not limited to the following: *Drunken Master*, *3 Evil Masters*, *Crippled Avengers*, *Super Power*, *36th Chamber of Shaolin*, *The 18 Bronzemen*, Unbeatable Shaolin, *7 Grandmasters*, *Mystery of Chessboxing*, *Five Deadly Venoms*, etc. As young kids in '70s and '80s, we were very inspired by all the martial arts films we watched, whether at the movie theaters or on TV. We were all very fortunate to have grown up during this era. Yup!

83. Sifu Jimmy Kung Fu, 1982

In 1982, I decided to join the local Boys & Girls Club. They had a big swimming pool. I loved going swimming and playing games with the other kids, games like Jaws or just racing one another across the pool. We also played table games upstairs—foosball, air hockey, ping-pong, eight-ball pool. We enjoyed many activities in the game room. Other times, we participated in basketball and dodgeball in the gym. I always got a good workout running back and forth in the gymnasium.

I started writing for a local newspaper. Their office was located inside the club. It was run by a local news editor named Mr. Gedgeway. He was very kind and helped kids improve their writing skills. I wrote several articles for the paper including a Roberto Clemente article and a story on nuclear weapons. I was awarded a Roberto Clemente record album ('78) and a book on the effects of nuclear explosions for my efforts. I was very happy with my awards.

The Boys & Girls club had a staff member named Jimmy. I think he was either Black or Puerto Rican. He taught kung fu classes on Saturdays at 12:00 p.m. Jimmy was a very cool person. I watched kung fu movies on TV every Saturday without missing a beat. They aired on channel 5 (WNEW) at 3:00 p.m. This class was perfect. I could train and then make it home on time to watch my martial arts movies. I began training with so much enthusiasm due to my motivation from watching all the films. My attendance was perfect. I religiously wore my kung fu pants and chinese slippers to every class. Week after week, Jimmy trained the students. He had us do horse stances and practice all sorts of techniques. I truly enjoyed his teaching methods. He was a good *sifu* (teacher). I found happiness in this new environment.

Tragically, it all came to an end. One day, I arrived early for class. Jimmy was nowhere to be found. The other martial arts students got tired of waiting and decided to go to the gym or the swimming pool. Jimmy was my sifu. I felt it was my duty as a student to wait until he arrived. I stretched a little and practiced a few movements. About two hours passed, and Jimmy never showed up. I was very worried about sifu and reluctantly gathered my things to leave the club. I started walking home wondering if sifu was okay.

As I reached the end of the block, I was utterly caught by surprise. I saw my trusted and honorable sifu Jimmy sitting on the porch of a house. To my shock and dismay, he was smoking a marijuana joint. Sifu was higher than a kite. He was startled when he saw me. After all, I was his most loyal and devoted student. We never spoke again after that. Sadly, it was the end of a beautiful relationship. Yup.

84. Hip-Hop Early Years, 1982

The year was 1982. Something large was brewing in the air. Breakdancing and electric boogie exploded on the scene. Radio stations 92 KTU, 98.7 Kiss FM, and 107.5 WBLS were all playing rap records—records like "The Message," "Sucker MCs," "Planet Rock," "Rockin' it," etc. A fever was building among the youth of the community. Breaking and popping was hot. Everyone wanted to be down. Wild Style, Style Wars, and eventually, Breakin' and Beat Street hit the theaters. Lee's, Nike Cortez, suede Pumas, shell-toe Adidas, mock necks, belt buckle nameplates, Playboy shoes, chinese slippers, and other forms of fashion became hip-hop must haves.

I started writing graffiti with my homeboys Ricky and Vinny. Ricky was Puerto Rican, and Vinny was Italian. They were mad cool and always up-to-date with the latest trends and so on. They were also b-boys. We started practicing together. They taught me helicopters, swipes, backspins, one-shot head spins, windmills (not continuous), hand spins, turtles, etc. We also practiced the electric boogie, a.k.a. popping. My brother Edward, who, at this time, preferred being called Edwin, was a good popper. He had a crew called Majestic Force with a bunch of his friends who also got down—Kevin, Ray, Ruben, Hanson, and several others. Edwin had a good friend named Luis who was a local DJ. He lived a few blocks from our house.

In the summer time, a block party would jump off at night. All the local crews and dancers would show up to battle. It was packed, and it was very difficult to see the battles. Everyone was hyped as the loud music blasted from the turntables and speakers. Lovebug Starski was very popular then. The song "You've Gotta Believe" was very popular among some of the dancers as they went at it. Everyone showed off their best moves, making sure not to get their fly clothes or sneakers dirty. The sweaters and T-shirts had names on the back representing your affiliation to a local crew or yourself.

In the winter, the jackets came on. The bombers and sheepskins were the most popular. Sneakers were adorned with fat laces, and Lee's pants had to have creases on the legs. Laces were wrapped around the bottom of our pants to simulate the kung fu movies we saw on TV or in the movie theaters. The *Five Deadly Venoms* were immensely popular back then, and our fashion matched the influence of what we were watching on film. Bruce Lee was also a major catalyst in the hip-hop realms. His energy and movements were mimicked by nearly every kid playing on the streets. Waya!

85. Luis, Mariano, 1982

I had two crazy friends growing up. They were brothers—the twins of sin, Luis and Mariano. Mariano was like the son of Satan. He was very sneaky and conniving and always looking for mayhem. He had a hairdo like the Bride of Frankenstein. Mariano could've been the poster boy for Mephistopheles. Luis on the contrary, had a very mellow personality and always followed his older brother's footsteps. They were my go-to buddies when I wanted to be mischievous. Between the three of us, we always got into trouble. We hung around our building in the backyard or alley quite often. Sometimes, we ventured off to the arcades to play video games. Once we were out of loot (money), we headed over to a highway nearby. We played chicken dodging out cars and trucks, a death-defying game, the stupid things that kids did and still do to this day. There was a patch of grass growing of the side of the hill from atop the highway. We flung ourselves of the hill on cardboard boxes at breakneck speed. We slid all the way to the service road on the bottom, trying to avoid the oncoming cars. This was a usual afternoon of play for us. My brother and his crazy-as-hell friend Jose would sometimes join us in the fun.

One day, we play wrestled in the grass, and things quickly got out of hand. We got into a silly dispute, and I ended up fighting both brothers back-to-back. After the fight, we dusted ourselves off, shook hands, and decided to be friends again. I mean, we could've gone our separate ways, but we really need one another for our naughty deeds. Halloween was the best time for us, especially mischief night, which fell on the day right before Halloween. Egg throwing was very popular among the youth, also ringing bells and then disappearing out of sight. Filling up old socks with baby powder and then whacking one another over the head was another activity we truly enjoyed. Throwing pebbles at passing cars and home windows was also on our to-do list. Lastly, making bonfires out of dry leaves and tree branches in the middle of the road was definitely a favorite. The fires stretched out for several blocks. We were very naughty boys. Mariano and Luis were two cool dudes. On Halloween day, we all suited up and went trick-or-treating to get as much candy as possible. My favorite costume was Dracula. I always felt he was smooth and debonair, and out of all the monsters, he was the most intelligent. If you lined him side by side with the Wolfman, Frankenstein, and the Mummy, he always stuck out. Fun times and crazy friends. Yup!

86. Mom Breakdown, 1982

In 1982, my cousins Angie, Betty, and Clarissa moved with our family to Main Street in Bridgeport, Connecticut. Angie arrived a few weeks earlier and was the oldest. Clarissa was the youngest. Their mom, Matilda, was my mother's older sister. It was extremely tight living in a small apartment all huddled together. Including my parents, Edward, and I, there were eight of us. Plus throw in my dog Chigui and the total was nine. Chigui was a very small cute black-and-white chihuahua. He was my little bud, my little companion. He enjoyed his usual dog food, but occasionally ate table scraps which included Doritos and Kraft slices of cheese. Chigui really loved Doritos. He would make loud crunching sounds with a grin on his face as he happily devoured them. At night, he slept on my bed by my feet. I loved that pooch! When times were really tough, I took my dog for a walk and told him all my problems. He was a great listener, even though he only responded by licking my face. Thank goodness he was always there when I really needed him.

The day after they arrived from Puerto Rico, I took Betty and Clarissa to a nearby playground. We played on the swings and slides. There was a rubber tire swing in the park that Clarissa really enjoyed as she swung back and forth in a moment of joy. Unbelievably, some young blond-haired girl kept eyeballing her from the slide. Clarissa didn't speak a word of English but felt the heat. Remarkably, they stared each other down like a boxing showdown for a championship fight. All of a sudden—ting, ting, ting—it was on. Without a single word uttered, the two girls started swinging for the fences. *Holy Mackerel!* I thought. There was so much vent-up rage inside the girls. I just couldn't believe it was happening. I was like "No way, Jose!" My cousin beat the girl into oblivion. Betty and I separated the two of them and then quickly left the park. We never returned to the playground.

Betty and Clarissa had a severe case of "menuditis." It was a crazy fan obsession with the young Puerto Rican pop-singing sensation group Menudo. The girls had tons of posters, magazines, buttons, pins, albums, and all other sorts of other memorabilia. They utterly drove me up the wall with their extreme fanaticism over the group. They were glued to the TV set every time Menudo came on. I guess it was the same for my aunt Matilda and Mom when the Beatles were popular in the 1960s. As adults, we could laugh at it now. All in all, it was cool having my cousins around, but it made food scarcer. We were already struggling before their arrival, but my parents always found a way to scrimp and save to buy groceries. Sometimes, mom would venture to the local food pantry to get powdered or canned carnation milk which tasted horrible. Around our house Tang, Kool Aid, and Sunny Delight were the drinks of choice instead of orange juice. It was much cheaper, and you could make gallons of the fake juice with tap water. The drinks always tasted sour and bitter no matter how much sugar you added. No frills Pathmark-brand cereals filled our shelves, instead of the more popular brands such as Frosted Flakes, Apple Jacks, or Fruity Pebbles. Canned hash browns, sausages, pork and beans, and cream of corn became a staple at our home. The food was utterly disgusting, but you had to make do with what you had. It was definitely a tough time to get through, but we always found a way to manage somehow.

One night, my parents got into a heated argument as they were very stressed from the situation we found ourselves in. I was only twelve years old at the time. Mom sadly had a nervous breakdown. She punched and shattered the window in the living room, cutting her hand and arm in the process. She suddenly took off running into the streets barefoot. I ran after her barefoot as well. The street was full of blood from the cuts on her arm and hand. I was so scared. I thought she must have severed a vein. She kept running and running as I screamed for her to stop. "Please, Mom, please stop!" I cried out. She didn't hear me because of her mental state at the time. Cars were zigzagging, trying to avoid her. Drivers beeped their horns. Finally, after an exhaustive run, she collapsed in a puddle of blood. I thought she was dead. I cried nonstop and quickly held her in my arms until the ambulance arrived. I said, "Mom, please don't die. Please don't die!" When the ambulance arrived, the paramedics put her on a stretcher and loaded her onto the vehicle. I jumped on the ambulance with her as it took off. My dad was nowhere to be found. *Where the hell is he, doesn't he care?* I thought in despair. I sobbed all the way to the hospital seeing my mom all bandaged up that way.

My heart was heavy. I love you, Mom. Eventually, my aunt found an apartment and moved out. Even though it was over crowded in the apartment, I must admit I did miss them when they left. Yup.

87. Mom, Atari 2600, 1982

In the early 1980s, my brother and I were addicted to the Atari 2600 video games. Like most kids at the time, we spent many hours trying to turn over the scores on the games. There was no memory card or save button back in those days. We constantly blasted one another to bits in the very fun military game called Combat. We both also spent a lot of time playing air and sea battle. Edward's favorite game hands down was Asteroids. He was a wizard in that game. He maneuvered his way around the screen with his little rocket ship, avoiding any collision with all foreign space particles. Any impact would have surely resulted in the destruction of his vessel. He thrusted himself around, forward and back and side to side on the screen with the help of his ship's rocket booster. Edward was brilliant in this game and was able to turn over the score several times. I, on the other hand, loved Space Invaders. All types of aliens marched themselves downward from the heavens to annihilate everything in their path. "Tum, tum, tum, tum, tum, tum, tum" was the sound they made as they sped up their attack. I blasted them one by one, wave after wave. I must say, I was very proficient in the art of destruction.

One late afternoon, I was on the console for hours at the point of turning over the game. You needed a score of 999,999. My brother was like, "Keep going! You got it!" I was amped up. I had 990,000 points, and I was on the verge of turning Space Invaders inside out. All of a sudden, from the nether regions of the kitchen, I could hear Mom calling me out for dinner. I was like, "Yeah, all right, Mom, I'll be there in a minute!"

"Hurry, or your food will get cold," she replied.

I turned a blind eye to her words and kept on blasting away. Edward was already seated for dinner. "Tum, tum, tum, tum, tum," the aliens kept coming. My score was rocketing 999,950...999,960...999,970... I was beaming with excitement. When suddenly—bam! I felt Mom yanking at my ear and pulling me away from the game unit and saying, "No te dije que vengas a comer!" translated "Didn't I tell you to come and eat!" She pulled the plug from the game, and that was that. I can't say I enjoyed dinner that night. Yup!

88. Two Good Friends, 1983–84

Two of my best friends growing up were Joseph "Cuchy" Martinez and Heriberto Soto. They were opposites to each other.

Cuchy loved to hang out and deejay while Heriberto loved staying home and playing video games. Cuchy had a beautiful turntable system. It included a pair of Technics turntables with a Gemini mixer and an amp with two very powerful speakers. He loved scratching and mixing records on them. He loved playing "Pump Me Up" by Grandmaster Melle Mel. He'd spent hours mixing back and forth with two copies of that record. "Pump, pump, pump, pump me up / XXXXXXXXX" over and over again. That tuned played in my head everywhere I went. He played that record so much that I felt nauseous every time I heard it. I was like "Yo, Cuchy, change the record already!" He then played "What People Do for Money." Cuchy hooked up the mic as I rapped or beatboxed over the instrumental side of the record. We had lots of fun. On weekends, we hit the mall to buy sneakers, shirts with old English lettering, and gold or silver nameplate belts. Cuchy's mom occasionally made food for us with a tall glass of soda on the side to quench our thirst. She was very nice.

I spent quite a bit of time on the other side of town at Heriberto's house playing Yar's Revenge, ET, Pitfall, Congo Bongo, Adventure, Venture, and Haunted House. Heriberto always gave me a glass of Kool-Aid every time I dropped by. He was very mellow by nature and always spoke with a lisp. He knew all the secret codes and mazes to the games. He collected video game books so that he could improve his scores. After we moved from Bridgeport, due to my pop's crazy antics, I never saw them again. Cuchy and Heriberto were two very cool dudes. I will never forget them.

89. Angie, Gang, 1983

My cousins moved across town to a rough and seedy neighborhood. I spent countless hours playing records at their house. "Thriller" by Michael Jackson was a favorite. We danced to all the classic songs from the album. Hip-hop recordings from artist like Grandmaster Flash, G.L.O.B.E. & The Whiz Kid, Run-DMC, and Afrika Bambaataa & the Soul Sonic Force were extremely popular at the time. I threw down many times busting out some of the latest B-boy breaking moves on numerous occasions. Angie was dating a kid named Lee. Now mind you, there were many kids nicknamed Lee in the neighborhood due to the Bruce Lee explosion in the movie theaters back in the 1970s–80s. Angie's boyfriend was a supercool cat who had a muscular build resembling Bruce Lee. Lee always wore a pair on Kung Fu pants, Chinese slippers, and a white muscle T-shirt. He always carried a pair of hardwood chucks with him. He was also a very good graffiti writer and DJ. He had a very nice turntable system. I'd go to his house and break while he was spinning on the wheels of steel. Jam Master Jay was one of my favorite records. I loved getting down to that song. That part "In '84 he will be a little faster and only packers make a real Jam Master!" drove me nuts. I furiously busted out some footwork and spun on my head and back. I always rocked my playboy shoes or Nike Cortez sneakers, which was great for breaking. Lee pants were the choice back then. Lees always had to have a sharp crease through the middle from ironing. Turtleneck shirts were popular back then as well. Burgundy was my favorite color. Burgundy Lees and turtleneck with gray Nike Cortez with a burgundy stripe on the side. Lee's brother was also a graffiti writer. He was much older, so we never hung out together. Lee and Angie eventually went their separate ways.

One day, on a warm afternoon, I decided to take a walk to my cousin's house for a visit. I loved taking long walks back then. As I made my way through town, I could hear music blaring from radios as people hung out. It was a great time for music. Cops didn't bother anyone for playing radios out loud. I was a few blocks from cousin's home when I heard a sudden news flash that the legendary crooner/singer Marvin Gaye had been shot to death by his own father. I loved his music. My heart sank not only for the loss of such a great artist but by the way he tragically died. I grew around domestic violence, and I had many deep buried feelings that came out when this happened. I finally reached my cousin's place. We didn't play any music. It was a very somber day.

On one nice summer night, Angie, my cousins Betty and Clarissa, and I were hanging out around a local parking lot. We were joking and chatting up a storm and just having some good ole fun. Angie was very funny and charming, and she always knew how to make us laugh. A young lady passed by. She and Angie gave each other a long not-so-friendly stare down and exchanged some not-so-kind words. Big mistake. The girl was part of a local gang called the Zapatas. Several minutes later, a whole mob of people started making their way down the block. I said, "Angie, run, let's get the hell out of here!" Betty and Clarissa quickly ran and hid behind some bushes. Angie was like "Nope, I'm not running!" I pleaded with her to hide. She stood her ground. She lit a cigarette and commenced smoking it. The mob was almost upon us. I quickly dived behind some bushes. The mob was about fifteen people deep. There were some big dudes and a couple of chicks in the crowd. Angie was sitting down when the girl approached her. (Remember, we were young kids and really couldn't do much, so we hid, which Angie should have done as well but was too stubborn for her own good.) The girl stood over her and looked down at Angie and said, "Talk some shit now, bitch! Angie just casually kept smoking her cigarette as if nothing had happened. She was totally surrounded by the gang now. The girl smacked her real hard as the cigarette went flying like a beacon of light into the darkness. "I thought so!" the girl yelled out. The rest of us made sure to stay out of sight. We wanted to help, but the odds were too great. We would've gotten smashed. The mob finally made their way out of the parking lot and slowly disappeared into the night. We came out of our hiding spots and said, "Why didn't you run!"

Angie nodded and said, "No!" Yup!

90. My Brother's Beating, 1983

I was awakened from my peaceful sleep early one summer morning in 1983. It was about 6:00 a.m. I heard a noisy commotion and Mom desperately screaming out loud. My nerves were rattled as I quickly jumped out of bed. "What the hell is going on!" I said. I heard my poor brother Edward's cries from the kitchen as he wailed out in pain. I thought, *Perhaps he burned himself making breakfast.* That wasn't the case.

To my astonishment, my dad was viciously beating him mercilessly across his body and face. My dad looked totally enraged like he was diabolically possessed. He beat him with one of my jump ropes. It was made of thick wooden handles, ball bearings, and a heavy nylon cord. The cord was tightly wrapped around Dad's large hands. Dad swung wildly as my poor, defenseless brother tried to cover up. He hit Edward with the wooden handles over and over again. I could hear the thuds the handles made upon impact with my brother's badly bruised body.

Mom yelled at Dad several times to stop and tried to intervene but was forcefully pushed away. Dad blindly continued his furious assault and pummeled my defenseless brother relentlessly until exhaustion. My brother cried in desperation and agony. I yelled and cried, "Leave him alone! Leave him alone!" The beating lasted for what seemed like an eternity, or approximately five minutes.

Horrendous! I was mortified. It was a new low for this monster. I was pissed and full of rage. My brother's arm was broken. "Fuck you, Dad, you motherfucker!" This irked my anger from a place deep inside me. From that day forward, I was resistant toward this tyrant we called Dad. That was the end of any good feelings I had toward this man. My brother cried and ran out of the house, never to return. My so-called dad, or monster, went back to sleep as though nothing had occurred. No compassion. No remorse. Nothing. Yup!

91. The Boogeyman, Eggy and I, 1983

Kids had a vivid imagination back in the days due to all the sci-fi and horror films of the 1950s–80s. We spent countless hours at the drive-ins and cinemas watching the latest zombie, supernatural, and low-budget slasher films of the era. Late night TV replayed classic monster films with notable actors such as Vincent Price, Christopher Lee, Don Chaney, Boris Karloff, Bela Lugosi, Peter Cushing, etc. Karen Black was also a staple on late nights as well. She had appeared in many films but most notably *Trilogy of Terror*, *Burnt Offerings*, and *The Strange Possession of Mrs. Oliver*. For many of us growing up during those years, horror was entrenched in our bones. We were scared out of our wits by watching these films, but I must admit we loved every minute of it.

Our playtime reflected what we were experiencing at the time. Naturally, we always tried spooking one another by jumping out of closets or from behind dark spaces. We also loved scaring one another with ghost stories and tales of the supernatural. Other times, we took things to another level by playing the Boogeyman. Our goal was to scare the hell out of one another. I had a creepy, diabolical mask left over from the previous Halloween that we used to play the game. We always played at nightfall. A bunch of kids gathered around my friend Edwin's house. There were many unkempt bushes surrounding his home, which made for a good game due to the fact that there were many places to hide. Most of the kids in the neighborhood were rather demented back then, perhaps due to watching to many grotesque movies of the sort. I usually started things off. Rule 1 was that you had to stay around the perimeter of the house. Rule 2 was don't get killed. I put on my mask and start counting backward in a bizarre-sounding voice, "Ten, nine, eight, seven..." The kids toke off in all directions in a frenzy. I based my body movements on the characters Michael Myers from *Halloween* and Jason from *Friday the 13th*. I walked slowly in a pacing manner around the house, breathing heavily and shuffling my footsteps. I could hear the kids hiding and whispering in the dark. I pretended that I didn't know where they were. It was part of my plan to scare the hell out of them. I quickly hid behind some bushes, waiting for the unsuspecting victims to come out of their safe little hiding spots, which sometimes took as long as five minutes. They made crinkling sounds as they stepped on dry leaves. I could hear them asking themselves, "Where is he, where is he? Oh my god, I'm so scared." I just waited a bit longer, letting the fear of the unknown salivate in their mouths and then with a heart-pulsating scare, I yelled out "Argh" as I jumped out of the bushes like a demon from the pits of damnation. Some of them fell on their knees in shock while others took off running. I shifted gears and raced after them, enjoying the utter rush I felt seeing them flee like rabbits. I really enjoyed this game immensely. My friend Edwin's little brother Eggy switched places with me and wore the mask. His style was different in that he based his character on the *Mad Man* movie. He started counting fast as the kids darted away from his realm of existence. He shot like an arrow through the yard, picking off his victims one by one, as others tried to find makeshift hiding spots. Eggy was fast as the wind. I was rather slick and was able to avoid his attacks by working my way through the shadows in a ninjutsu fashion. I laughed inside, hearing him dismantling off one kid after another. After the game, we all laughed and went our separate ways. A good night of fun and scares. Yup!

92. East Side Middle School, 1983

I started attending East Side Middle School when I was thirteen. I loved this school. It was like *Fast Times at Ridgemont High*. My brother attended Harding High, which was on the other side of town. I rode the yellow bus to class every morning. Most of my friends and homeboys attended the same school. The classes were very interesting, and the teachers took time to help students. It was a great school. Unfortunately, it was built on top of a swamp and was gradually sinking year by year—at least that was the story that we were told.

I was a very studious kid. I strived to get As in all my classes. The situation at home was very unstable and unsettling and, at times, extremely disturbing. But nevertheless, I hit the books and made sure that I passed all my classes. I always sat in front of the class so that I wouldn't miss the lesson. I was a Goody Two-shoes so to speak. One girl named Eileen always sat in front of the class right next to me. She was my bitter rival to the end. We both were definitely the teacher's pets. Every time the teacher asked a question, both our hands shot up. It was like Arnold Horshack in the *Welcome Back, Kotter* TV show. "Oh, oh, oh, oh, oh, Mr. Kotter, I know!" he always shouted. We were both very competitive and wanted to be the best student. Eileen was rather annoying at times, but I respected how smart she was.

One morning, I barely missed the bus to school. The school was about two miles away. I decided then and there to run to school as fast as I possibly could. I had a Nike windbreaker jacket on, which made me sweat profusely, but I didn't care. I was always looking for an opportunity to work out. I was a pretty fast runner. I made it to school on time. The problem was that now, I was totally drenched in sweat. I entered the classroom like a ninja in the shadows and sat way in the back so that, in turn, no one would notice me. I took off my jacket and was totally caught off guard and embarrassed when big-mouthed Eileen in the front shouted, "Ew, what's that smell?" I tried making myself smaller and sunk myself underneath the desk. I worriedly thought, *Please shut up, big mouth!* I wasn't so lucky. Eileen yelled out across the sea of students who were all lined up in very neat rows and said, "Is that you, Anthony Colon?"

"Damn!" I said to myself. What irritated me the most was that she blurted out my first and last name. Now everybody knew it was me. I was only thirteen and was rapidly becoming a young man. I forgot to do one of the most important things that morning, and that was to wear my deodorant. You better believe I had never forgotten to wear it again. Lesson learned. Ha ha.

I shared another class with my homeboys Ricky and Vinny. These were the two guys who taught me how to break (a.k.a. break-dance) in 1982. They also wrote wild style graffiti. The *Style Wars* hip-hop documentary aired on PBS one evening. The next day, all the kids in class were doing burners (freestyle art) on paper. Ricky absolutely had the best style when it came to writing (graffiti). I loved writing and spent quite a bit of time practicing the art form. I did some artwork for my brother and his friends from high school. Ray, Ruben, and Luis were part of my brother's crew. I used to hang out and spend time with them dancing. They were poppers (electric boogie), and I mostly breaked (breakdanced). I used to go with them to the mall all the time to check out the latest fashions. They were cool guys.

The lunchroom at East Side Middle was a madhouse. Kids were always horse playing or cracking jokes. Food was constantly being hurled across the tables. Boys pulled on the girls' long hair, especially if they had crushes on them. This was their way of saying "I like you." Friday was always the best. It was pizza day in the lunchroom. Kids merrily chomped away on their slices. Yum, yum.

There were a lot of hot tempers at East Side Middle School. Sometimes, kids got heated, and things quickly got of hand. I guess kids were going through the effects of puberty and mood swings. They were many fights, mostly on the school bus and off the school grounds. My close friends Edwin Quiniones and Carlos Nieves had a total of three fights. The first time Carlos punched Edwin in the face, he was coming off the bus, giving him a black eye. The second time, Edwin returned the favor and did the same thing. The third time was a tie. Carlos also fought a kid named Kevin, who was a good popper (dancer). Carlos and Kevin had a few words on the bus. Kevin was much bigger than Carlos, but Carlos had a big heart and didn't back down. They went at it at the bus stop. Carlos got the first big punch in. Kids were always fighting back then.

One of my saddest memories from East Side Middle involved a tragic death. A teenager named Santos, who was in the eighth grade was shot and killed by a police officer. He was running from a crime scene. He was stealing hub caps. He was intervened by the police officer who gave chase and shot the young man in his back. The victim was only fifteen years old. Tragic. Yup.

93. Kung Fu Fever, 1970s–80s

It was the 1970s. The hit single "Kung Fu Fighting" was released on the radio. Bruce Lee was the undisputed king of kung fu cinema. People were in a frenzy. *The Big Boss*, *The Chinese Connection*, *Return of the Dragon*, and *Enter the Dragon* broke several box-office records worldwide and catapulted Bruce Lee to superstardom. Unfortunately, he didn't live long enough to enjoy his incredible success. Tragically, Bruce Lee died on July 20, 1973. From 1974–1984, movie theaters replayed the best of Bruce Lee's films. The classic 1960s *Green Hornet* TV series was mashed together into a two-hour movie.

Shortly after his passing, every little dragon copycat wannabe imaginable came out of the woodwork. Bruce Liang, Bruce Lo,

Dragon Lee, Bruce Le, Bruce Li, and many others tried their best to imitate the master. One person from the mix rose to the surface. His name was Bruce Li. He was most undoubtedly the best and most revered of the impostors. Bruce Li quickly developed a large fan base that craved more from their deceased hero. Li mimicked Lee's movements and unique cat-like sounds. Li was very athletic, had great martial arts skills, and was able to fill a void at least temporarily for a majority of the fans.

Jackie Chan also got into the mix of things, trying his hand at being Bruce, but was coldly received by the public. He eventually found his niche and success in the comedic opera style of kung fu films. *Drunken Master*, *Fearless Hyena*, and *Snake in the Eagle's Shadow* became box office hits for Jackie Chan. A new star was born. Chuck Norris and Jim Kelly were also extremely popular in the martial arts movie industry. They produced several classic films in between them.

Ninja films starring Sho Kosugi became all the craze in the 1980s. Sho Kosugi showcased his wide array of exhilarating martial arts techniques that demonstrated the art of stealth on the silver screen for all to see. Kids were running around everywhere in mock ninja uniforms with wooden swords in hand, playing out their movie fantasies. Later on, *The Karate Kid* exploded into movie theaters with the now legendary Mr. Miyagi and Daniel LaRusso as the main characters. This epic movie highlighted the relationship between student and sensei. Wax on, Wax off! Pat "Noriyuki" Morita was nominated for an Oscar for best supporting actor for his portrayal.

Local television stations throughout the country played Shaw Brothers kung fu films on weekends, creating a mass following. The *Five Deadly Venoms*, *The 36th Chamber of Shaolin*, *Instructors of Death*, *The Deadly Mantis*, *Street Gangs of Hong Kong*, *Chinatown Kid*, *Chinese Super Ninjas*, *When Taekwondo Strikes*, *Mad Monkey Kung Fu*, *Heroes of the East*, and many more classics played on the tube every Saturday afternoon. The drive-in movie aired on New York's Channel 5.

The 1970s saw an emergence of fanatics who wanted to learn martial arts or be the next Bruce Lee. Kung fu shops sprouted up everywhere. They sold chinese slippers, nunchakus, ninja stars, kung fu and karate suits, Bruce Lee posters, martial arts books and magazines, weapons, heavy bags, and all sorts of training gear. I myself had several favorite martial arts spots that I frequented regularly in NYC: Tiger Kim's martial arts supplies on the Grand Concourse in the Bronx, Bok Lei Tat (Bruce Lee / Chuck Norris sign) on Canal Street in Chinatown, Crown store in the middle of Forty-Second Street right next to the kung fu movie theaters, Jerome Avenue and Fordham Road kung fu shop underneath the elevated 4 Train, Jamaica Avenue kung fu shop, Yan Wah martial arts supplies near Fresh Pond Road in Queens, Honda Martial Arts on Twenty-Third street in Manhattan, Kinji San in Brooklyn, and countless others.

Dojos were packed with students who wanted to be able to move like their screen heroes or at least have the ability to defend themselves on the dangerous streets. Weirdos also came out claiming to be the masters of a secret art or falsely proclaiming to have incredible skills such as the death touch, etc. Martial arts fanatics made pilgrimages to the Forty-Second Street kung fu movie theaters, Chinatown kung fu movies theaters, and local neighborhood theaters to get their martial arts fix. Many people, including myself, wore kung fu suits and chinese slippers as part of our everyday wardrobe. I always concealed a pair of chucks inside my pants. I copied this by watching Bruce Lee subduing his opponents in his films by whipping out his weapons and letting loose. Bruce Lee was the man and always will be. Everybody wanted to be him. This style of dress became extremely popular in the early days of hip-hop among the old school B-boys. Waya! Yup!

94. Puerto Rico and Grandpa, 1984

Due to my parents' marital problems, Mom and I took off for Puerto Rico in May 1984. I had just turned fourteen years old. I was in the eighth grade. I was attending East Side Middle School in Bridgeport, Connecticut. I was doing pretty well in all my classes despite my situation at home. Unfortunately, I didn't attend graduation with all my other classmates. My teachers realized the predicament I was in, so they agreed to promote me to the ninth grade even though I was absent for the last few weeks of class.

I was attending the Tao Te Ching Institution of Martial Arts during this unsettling time. It was located near Seaside Park in Bridgeport. I had some close training buddies, which included Jay, Melvin, Marcos, and others. My teachers were very kind and under-standing—Sensei Cornell, Michael, and Harry. On my last day of class, we took some pictures in front of the school. Unfortunately, my mom lost her camera with the undeveloped pictures still inside of it. It was the very last time I saw any of my martial arts classmates.

Mom and I were all packed for our trip to Puerto Rico. It had been seven years since we last visited the island. I was very excited and happy for us. We were finally getting away from all the carnage at home. My uncle Paul dropped us off at the airport. I felt that this was a new beginning for us, a new life. The first few days in Puerto Rico were great. Mom and I spent time with the family. We stood at my uncle Isaiah's (Cholo) home. My uncle had me accompany him on early morning runs in his pickup truck. He sold fruit all over town from his vehicle. He taught me how to use the PA system. I firmly said, "Guineos maduro cinco libras por un peso!" which meant "Five pounds of bananas for only one dollar!" My uncle Cholo drove up and down some winding mountain roads. The roads were very nar-row. He drove fast, and at times, I felt like the truck was going to skid off the mountain and crash into the valley below. It was a harrowing experience. I'm glad I'm alive and was able to write about today.

Most of the time, Mom ran around with my uncle and aunt doing errands. I played with my cousins Michelle, Isaiah Jr., and Irene. We played games, watched TV, and listened to all kinds of music. But what I truly enjoyed was training in the martial arts. I practiced my techniques by repeatedly kicking at my uncle's banana tree in the backyard, eventually knocking it over. He wasn't too happy about that. My uncle Cholo told my uncle Luis, who lived further down the road, about the banana tree mishap. My uncle Luis laughed and said, "I will take him to a real karate school so that he can train properly." My uncle Luis was married to my aunt

Candita. My aunt Candita was a seamstress, and my uncle made and sold shampoo.

One night, my uncle Luis and I decided to go for a drive. We visited several martial arts schools in the area. We finally arrived at one school that taught kung fu. I was very excited. I hadn't trained in a school for a few months. My uncle spoke to the teacher. My uncle said, "El tiene gije de karate, lo que quiero saber es, si el sabe karate de verdad," which meant "He has karate fever, I want to know, if he really knows karate." The stern teacher allowed me to train that night with the adults' class. It was going to be a test of my skills. It was "put up or shut up" time, but I was ready to back it up. The teacher started the class with a basic warmup. We did several calisthenic exercises, and then we did some stretches as well. Now it was time for sparring. I really loved to fight at this point. I really didn't care too much for kata training. I didn't realize the value of kata training until later on.

The sifu paired everyone off with a partner. We then started with some light fighting drills as the contact gradually got heavier and heavier. We all broke a sweat since it was very hot and humid that night. The teacher had me fight everyone in the class back-to-back with no rest. This wasn't a problem for me. I used to run and workout every day. My endurance was very high. I was young and strong, and it really didn't faze me. I used my patented Bruce Lee side kick, like the one Lee used on O'hara in *Enter the Dragon*. I knocked a few guys across the room this way. The sifu really was pissed off. He must've thought, *How dare this young punk disrespect my school!* Mind you, I wasn't trying to be disrespectful. That was never my intention. I was just a young kid trying to defend himself by all means. The teacher angrily said, "Now you and me!" We went at it, which I must admit I held my own. This really got his fire going. The sifu lost his cool and challenged me to fight him outside. I thought, *This guy is nuts; he's losing it.* My uncle Luis spoke to him and calmed him down. I was rather upset and perplexed by the situation I found myself in due to my uncle's bizarre antics. He made it up to me by getting me a few cheeseburgers and a strawberry milkshake at McDonalds. My crazy uncle Luis (RIP). Yup!

A few weeks after arriving in Puerto Rico, Mom decided to go back to New York without me. She said, "I have to take care of a few things. I will see you soon, my son." I was very upset. I didn't want Mom to get hurt again. I tried pleading with her to stay, but it was not to be. Mom gave me a few bucks, and off she went. This was a very painful time in my life for me. Here I was, a fourteen-year-old kid stuck in Puerto Rico without my parents, brother, and my friends. I tried to make the best of it. The first thing I did was go shopping to the Plaza Carolina mall. I bought several knickknacks and some food. I bought an *Inside Kung Fu* magazine with William Cheung on the cover. William Cheung was the gentleman who brought Bruce Lee to learn from Yip Man. Cheung was a senior student under him. I loved reading the magazine from front to back, including all the articles and the fine print.

To forget my problems, I spent a lot of time running through the hills of Puerto Rico. The sun was unrelenting and unforgiving. I brought all my martial arts gear with me to the island, including some spiffy kung fu boots that I had purchased back home. I wore these on my long runs. It left my feet very sore and calloused. I did my calisthenics daily, including pushups and jumping jacks. I stretched out every day as well. I was so inspired by Bruce Lee that I tried mimicking his movements and body gestures. Every few days, Mom sent me letters in the mail with some cash wrapped in tin foil. I used the money to buy all types of snacks in the local bodega (grocery store). I stocked up on cookies, chips, fruit juice, etc. It was a very long walk to the store, and I wasn't used to the sweltering heat of the tropics, but the snacks made me feel better now that I was all alone.

My mom's elder brother Mario decided to let me help him run his fruit stand. It was near a local freeway. The stand was stationed near the exit ramp lights. My uncle peddled all types of fruits. He also sold boxed glazed donuts. He taught me how to hustle and make a quick buck. As cars pulled off the freeway, I'd walk up to them and sell the items. It was tough working in the heat. My hair sizzled underneath the scorching tropical sunshine. I was always sweaty and thirsty. At the end of the day, my uncle blessed me with a few bucks for my hard work. My uncle Mario (RIP) was always very fair with me.

By this time, I was staying with my grandfather. He lived in an old two-story home. We both watched wrestling on TV. My grandfather was a huge fan. *Titanes en el Ring* was the top wrestling show on Puerto Rican television at the time. My grandpa got very excited during the matches and bounced around the sofa with sheer enthusiasm. He was in his eighties but still exhibited the energy of a person half his age. My grandfather's name was Hipolito Sanchez. He was very strict at times. He woke up every day at 4:00 a.m., but I'd still be resting in bed covered by a net to keep the mosquitos and bugs off me. My grandpa yelled from the kitchen, "Get up! It's time to work!" I thought in a sleepy state, *Seriously, old man, it's 4:00 a.m.!* He started making coffee with some coffee beans from his farm. Bam, bam, bam pounced off my ears as he slammed a mallet mashing and grounding the coffee. A few minutes after, the aroma of fresh brewed coffee percolated all through the house.

Unable to get some sleep, I got up and had my breakfast. It was a piece of toast with some cheese and a cup of joe. Back home, I was used to eating my morning cereal—Fruit Loops, Apple Jacks, Frosted Flakes, and other sweet, sugary delights. My grandfather was very strict and old-fashioned. He made certain that I helped around the house with duties. One morning, I was awoken by the sound of someone with a shovel, making a loud racket. I was like, "What the hell!" I walked out to the front porch of the house only to see my grandpa mixing a batch of cement. I thought, *This old guy is off his rocker!* He turned and looked at me with a steely look in his eyes and said, "Well, what the hell are you waiting for? Get down here!" The verdict was in; now I was sure he was insane. I took my sweet time, and he yelled out, "Hurry up, don't be lazy!"

"Gesh," I said under my breath. We spent several hours under the hot, unyielding Caribbean sun plying our craft. We built a cement wall around the house, brick by brick—no breaks, no rest, no time-outs until we accomplished our task. I must admit, I had a newfound respect for my grandpa. He was tough as nails, and boy, was he shrewd.

After spending several hours laboring around the house, now it was time to relax. My grandfather had a soft side to him after all. He gave me all types of fruits from his farm. Bananas were my favorite. He then proceeded to play one of his accordions. He was a very accomplished musician and took great joy and pride in playing his instrument. He played his songs with a wide grin on his face. I felt really good inside knowing that we shared a moment of happiness together. Grandpa (RIP). Yup! Ironically, now many years later, my mom resides in the home as a senior citizen of the island.

95. Bronx and Breaking, 1984

I returned to New York from Puerto Rico early in the summer of 1984. Mom, my aunt Matilda, and cousins Betty and Clarissa picked me up at JFK Airport. The first question I asked them was "What's playing in the movie theaters?" They responded, "*Ghostbusters, Gremlins, Beat Street, The Karate Kid,* and *Breakin'.*" *Cool,* I thought. We all boarded the car and headed back home to Bridgeport, Connecticut.

I was worried about my family situation at home. Mom and Dad were on the verge of a major breakup. They were constantly fighting with no end in sight. After several violent exchanges between them, Mom decided to leave Dad and go her separate way. Mom and I packed up all our personal belongings, preparing to leave the city of Bridgeport forever. There was one big problem: my brother, Edward, was in a foster home at the time. I hadn't seen my brother in a few months. I was very happy to see him. I told Mom, "Edward is going with us, right?"

Mom sadly replied, "Unfortunately, there is no space for him where we are going."

I was so angry. My heart was broken. My brother was my mentor and taught me so many things through the years. We were inseparable growing up. I was pissed off. Saying goodbye to my brother was one of the hardest things I'd ever had to do in my life. Not a day went by that I didn't think about him. He was always in my prayers. I felt deep inside my heart that I would one day see him again.

Mom and I ended up in the Bronx. We stayed at a friend's apartment for a few weeks on University Avenue near the Reservoir. Her name was Ruby, and her husband was Max. Well, we actually stayed with Ruby's cousins. They were diabetics and were always shooting up with needle, getting their insulin fix. It totally creeped me out. There was a major hospital strike in NYC in 1984. Due to the walkout, there was a massive nursing shortage. Mom started working at a nearby hospital as a nurse. Mom made quite a bit of money working a lot of overtime. She crossed the picket lines against the will and anger of all the striking nurses. But we needed the money. So Mom did what she had to do.

There was a sneaker store on Kingsbridge Road and Jerome Avenue owned by Asians. Mom bought me some cool sneakers and windbreaker jackets there. During this time, she purchased a beautiful boom box as a gift for me. After shopping, we always ended up eating at a nice local Chinese restaurant. I loved spending time alone with Mom. It meant a lot to me. She had gone through so much and was trying to get her life together. I totally respected her for that. Eventually, we packed up and left the University Avenue apartment and moved to Briggs Avenue by Kingsbridge Road. We crashed with my uncle Paul and his roommate Carmen on the first floor. My uncle Paul was a nurse too and also worked as a lifeguard on Orchard Beach. Carmen was in the New York City Police Academy, studying to become a law enforcement officer.

They were rarely home. The apartment was very small. It was very crowded and uncomfortable. Mom and I slept on the cold hardwood floor. It was okay, but I missed Edward so much. I tried making peace with my guilty conscience knowing that we had to leave Bridgeport. It was an emergency. Dad, in his crazy drug stupor, had become increasingly violent and unstable. I spent a lot of time alone watching TV, trying to get over my bitter feelings. A few weeks later, a lady upstairs who knew my uncle decided to move out of the building. Rachel and her baby son named Charlie. The apartment became available, so we moved upstairs to the second floor.

I hung around my new neighborhood trying to make friends. My first new friend was a kid named Johnny who lived downstairs. I was fourteen years old and was shocked that Johnny was only fifteen and had a superthick mustache. It was very similar to the one that Burt Reynolds, Robert Redford, and Billy Dee Williams had. Johnny always wore army fatigue pants. I always rocked a kung fu suit with chinese slippers and wrapped my pant bottoms with shoe laces just like the Five Deadly Venoms in the Shaw Brothers kung fu films. I also carried a pair of metal-studded nunchakus that my mom gave me for Christmas in 1983. I loved those chucks. Sometimes, Johnny and I played our boom boxes in the hallway. I breaked (breakdanced) on the hard marble floor. It was great for spinning moves. I got down and busted out backspins, one shot head spins, and handglides to the music of "F4000" by the Fearless Four, "It's Yours" by T La Rock, "A.M/P.M." by Dr. Jekyll & Mr. Hyde, "Beat Street" by Melle Mel, the Fat Boys/Disco 3, "Request Line" by Rock Master Scott & the Dynamic Three, "Masters of the Scratch" by Master O.C. & Krazy Eddie, and hip-hop mixes from radio stations 92 WKTU, 98.7 Kiss FM, and 107.5 WBLS.

I made my rounds on the block and other adjoining blocks as well, trying to familiarize myself with the area. There were a few game rooms nearby. The closest one was on my block right next to a Chinese restaurant. Track and Field and Jungle Hunt were the best games in that spot. On the opposite corner near Poe Park, there was another game room. The best game in that joint was Punch Out. I spent hours playing it. Down the block from there was a Pizzeria that had a cool video game called Space Ace. It had the same look as Dragon's Lair. These two games looked like real cartoons and were amazing and ahead of their time.

I spent a lot of time at the local Chinese restaurant. I often bought four chicken wings for a dollar. I loaded them with soy sauce, duck sauce, and hot sauce. I occasionally ate egg rolls which only cost fifty cents. I washed it all down with a cold soda. I burned it all off by breaking (breakdancing) in front of a church that was across the street from my building. I always used cardboard boxes to practice my spinning moves. Feeling motivated, I practiced my martial arts kicks as well and swung my chucks around like Bruce Lee in his films. I blasted my boom box as loud as I could for all to hear. There was a lady who lived on the first floor right next door to Johnny. She always played music out of her window. She was a big Prince fan. Prince had just released the *Purple Rain* album. It was a mega hit. I asked her, "Could you play some Michael Jackson songs." She flatly denied. She hated Michael Jackson and said, "He's in the closet and isn't real!" She was cool, a really nice person. She played "High Energy" a few times. It was a great dance single. Good times! For the life of me, I can't remember my friend's name.

On certain days, I'd walk up to Kingsbridge Road near the Grand Concourse checking out all the local shops. I searched for martial arts stores. There was a kung fu shop further down by Fordham Road and Jerome Avenue. It was underneath the elevated 4 Train. It was one of my favorite spots, and I spent plenty of time there. Tiger Kim's martial arts store was further down by the Concourse. They had tons of supplies. The RKO movie theater, Loews movie theater, and Alexander's department store were all on the Concourse. Crazy Eddie electronics and the VIM clothing store was further down on Fordham Road near Webster Avenue. VIM's had *Beat Street* movie posters all over its walls. The New York City Breakers were popular in the neighborhood. I heard they used to hang out by Poe Park and always did my best to meet them but unfortunately never did. I guess they were on tour back then. I spent many days surveying the area. Tiger Kim's dojo was on the opposite side of his store. It was underneath a movie theater. I stood in front of the school many times, gazing at the students' training pictures. There was one picture that fascinated me. It had showed all the students doing full chinese side splits. "Wow!" I said to myself in amazement. I took in a few movies back then. I saw the *Karate Kid* and *Ninja III: The Domination*. I paid only two dollars to watch these films at the RKO theater. I sat down with my popcorn and soda, enjoying my martial arts movies. I was the only person in the theater. It was a matinee.

Whenever I had a few bucks left, I munched out at a pizzeria on Kingsbridge Road. After downing a few cheesy slices, I played some of the video games that they had on the premises. St. James Park was nearby. There was a graffiti burner on the sign entering the park. The sign was above the entrance walkway. It spelled out *St. James Park*.

The piece was beautiful and had many vivid colors with painted bricks around it. I'd sit on the park bench for hours thinking about my personal family problems. I daydreamed quite a bit back then. I watched squirrels playing in the grass and people playing handball and paddleball on the courts nearby. I tried reading some of the tags on the walls. Menace Mel, Haz, and Cope 2 were some of the names I could barely make out.

Feeling bored, I practiced my martial arts techniques, kicking and leaping into the air. A young teen approached me asking all sorts of questions. He went by the name Ninja. He had some slick moves. Backflips were his specialty. He rocked a super-fly windbreaker jacket. He was very cool and used to break too. I also met a muscle-bound, cock-diesel guy named Conan. He always drank a forty-ounce bottle of beer, a Colt 45 malt liquor. He was mad cool as well. I also met a very friendly girl named Sarina who lived on Valentine Avenue. On one hot summer night, Ninja and I got down on the concrete and showed off our best dance skills. The crowd watched as we did our coolest maneuvers. For weeks after, we kept practicing our breaking moves every night on the block. Every Saturday night, we listened and danced to the mega mixes on WBLS, WKTU, and Kiss FM. The DJs went off spinning the best hip-hop records of the era.

One Saturday night, Ninja and I got into a heated breaking battle. We got caught up in the moment. There was a crowd checking us out. It didn't help that Sarina was present. I think Ninja had a thing for her. He did his moves and got some claps from the small crowd. He did some backflips, swipes, etc. I wasn't one to be denied, so I ripped off some of my own moves. I did swipes as well but added a one-shot head spin on the street pavement. Concrete! No hat. No protection. I spun about three or four times. The battle was intense—well, at least for the two of us, two young bucks from the Bronx who felt an intense urge to prove themselves. Neither one of us wanted to submit to the other. After the battle, we exchanged some heated words. We were both very angry. He said, "Watch your back!"

I responded, "No, you watch your back!"

We both looked at each other with disdain and angrily marched in separate directions.

The very next day, I found myself practicing my breaking moves on Briggs Avenue in front of a Catholic school. The school was right across the street from the building I lived in. I was preparing myself in case I had to battle Ninja again. I was wearing my frog button kung fu suit and white-bottomed chinese slippers. I had my nunchakus tucked in my back pants for security. My head crackers. As I was throwing down on the cardboard, I felt someone was watching me. I looked over my shoulder and glanced over at the stranger. I rapidly stood up as he approached me. I took a guarded stance. He said, "Yo, you talking to my girl?"

My mind started racing. I tried remembering if I talked to any girls lately. Lost in thought, I quickly responded, "Who's your girl?"

"Janec!" I heard him blurt out. A few days prior, I started talking to Janec, not realizing she had a boyfriend. I only told one other person of our secret rendezvous: Ninja. He must've ratted me out to this punk. That dirty, no-good, good-for-nothing backstabber. "I didn't know she had a man," I responded, keeping my distance. We were standing in front of a Chinese restaurant when, all of a sudden, all hell broke loose, and he swung wildly at me.

My martial arts training kicked in. I got the best of him by punching him in the face several times. I was really strong from all the breaking and karate training. Plus, no punk was going to walk me down. *Hell nah*, I thought. We both ended up wrestling on the ground. The Chinese restaurant workers were yelling at us out loud in Chinese, swinging a broom. They probably cursed us out. I don't blame them. Having fights in front of the restaurant must be bad for business. He-he. The punk tried wrapping both his legs around my neck. Pissed off at his antics, I mustered up the strength to break free and mounted him and then proceeded to grab his head with my hands and slammed his skull into the concrete floor a few times. I followed the assault with a punch to his face. My right fist slammed into his cheek and slid right off. We were both drenched in sweat, and his face was very slippery. My fist hit the cement as it cracked. My hand was broken, but I seriously didn't give a damn. So be it. I slammed his head into the sidewalk one final time for good measure. We got up and dusted ourselves off. No words were exchanged as we both went our separate ways, but I knew what was up. I quickly left the area and called my mom from a phone booth a block away. I was in the middle of explaining to her what just happened when a group of thugs from Valentine Avenue suddenly came marching down the block. They didn't see me, as I hid behind the booth. They all gathered in front of my building about ten deep. My mom said, "Go stay with your cousins Paulie and Sammy." My cousins lived a few blocks away on Decatur Avenue. I quickly did a disappearing act. When I reached my cousins' home, I told my aunt Aly the reason for my unexpected visit. She welcomed me with open arms. I spent the night joking around with my cousins and watching the classic TV shows *The Honeymooners* and *Star Trek*, eventually dozing off.

The next morning, we all woke up. Duke, the family dog, made his morning rounds enthusiastically licking everyone's faces. The whiff of his early morning breath was definitely an eye-opener. We all gathered around the TV and watched cartoons as each one of us ate a bowl of cereal for breakfast. My hand was very swollen at this point. I wasn't going to the hospital. I hated hospitals. I'd spent too much time there. I was like "To hell with that, I'm going to let it heal by itself!"

A few hours later, a bunch of us kids headed down to Webster Avenue. There was an overpass for cars nearby. On one side of the overpass were several trees lined up side by side. The drop from the overpass to the ground was about twenty-five feet. One by one, we all jumped from the overpass to the trees and scaled are way down. Like well-trained ninjas, we achieved our mission. I was able to do this despite my injured hand. The crew of Decatur Avenue kids were made up of myself, Carlos, Jose, Ismael, Robert, Alex, Ruben, and my cousins Paulie and Sammy (RIP).

It was a nice sunny day, and I was feeling pretty good. We all took off and marched down Webster Avenue. We gathered near the Amtrak train yards. Several rock formations lined the side of the tracks. Jose was the first one of us to successfully climb and conquer a large rock wall that day. We had a rope, which we tossed up to

Jose. I shouted up at him, "Tie the rope around a tree! Make sure that it's secure!"

He shouted down, "Okay!"

It was a great plan, but there was one problem: Jose never learned the ABCs of making knots. As my luck would have it, I was the next one in line to climb the rockies. My hand was throbbing from the pain from the previous night's fight. But I toughened it out and made my way to the top with just one hand. I felt a moment of overwhelming pride as I was about to reach the summit of my valiant effort. As I peeked over the edge of the cliff, I tugged on to end of the rope very tightly. Suddenly, my heart sank into the pit of my stomach as I saw the rope violently untangling itself from the tree.

The last thing I remember was the awkward look of surprise on Jose's face as I fell backward. I hit my head on the way down, against the jagged rocks, sustaining a massive concussion to my head. I was knocked out cold. I was unconscious for several minutes. According to witnesses, which included my cousins Sammy (RIP) and Paulie, I rose to my feet after a few minutes and started walking up the block totally drenched in blood. They said, "We tried to help you, but you cursed us out, yelled 'Don't touch me,' and passed out again!" I was laid out in the middle of the street till the ambulance arrived. On the way to the hospital, I recalled being awoken by the extremely bright sunlight that shined through the back window of the ambulance. I took a quick glimpse of the paramedics as they worked feverishly over my battered body before passing out a third time.

At the hospital, doctors attended to my severe injuries. The doctors informed my poor distraught mother that I had a broken right hand, a concussion, and two lower spinal vertebrae hairline fractures. I was in the hospital for two weeks. Luckily for me, my spinal cord wasn't damaged from the fall. I asked my doctor, "Will I be able to breakdance or practice karate again?" The look on the doctor's face said it all. He responded, "I don't think so." I stared at him like he was nuts. Totally bonkers! The doctors ran several tests on me daily, probing, pinching, and jabbing my legs with their devices. Lying in bed was torture. I was too hyper, but the pain was unbearable every time I tried walking to the bathroom.

I watched tons of cartoons on the hospital TV set. A young boy was placed in the bed next to me. He was so annoying. We both had remote controls and were always dueling for which show to watch. He smiled at me and chuckled every time he changed the channel. Boy, I wished I had a slingshot back then. *Bam!* I thought. I was finally discharged from the hospital. The doctors said, "You need plenty of rest." They recommended that I sleep on the floor for some time till my back healed. My wonderful family—Mom, Aunt Aly, Sammy (RIP), and Paulie—took great care of me. They catered to my every whim. I love them all.

Ironically, three weeks later, I was rushed to the hospital once again. One afternoon, I felt very nauseous. I was hunched into a ball most of the day. I was vomiting relentlessly. The smell of my hungry cousins cooking Ooodles of Noodles got under my skin and turned my stomach upside down. Mom soon returned from work and realized something wasn't right. I didn't greet her at the door as part of my usual routine. She placed her hand on my forehead, checking for a fever. She got on the phone and called an ambulance. The paramedics arrived and checked my vital signs. One of them suggested that I might have a flu and should just sleep it off. Mom worked in a hospital herself. She was experienced in these matters. "Nope, take my son to the hospital," she adamantly said. I was taken to North Central Bronx Hospital. The doctor's prognosis was that I had a case of appendicitis. I was operated on that same night. Thank goodness. Mom was right. Mom knows best! Yup!

96. Street Fights, 1984

Growing up in the 1970s and 1980s, you simply had to know how to fight. Out in the streets, you couldn't be no sucker, chump, punk, wuss, sissy, toy, or mama's boy. Neighborhood hoodlums would test you at any moment. Sometimes you were pushed to the edge or over it. Put your dukes up and come out swinging. No one wanted to be a pushover. Hell nah!

Pick up a stick, brick, bottle, or whatever and crack someone across the head. Earn your respect. Act like a maniac and nobody messed with you. My brother helped me out of a lot of fixes, but I was alone more often than not. By the time I was fourteen years old, I had at least ten street altercations in which I broke my hand, had my head cracked wide open, had busted lips, a busted eye, and several bruises.

Unfortunately, I was jumped several times in elementary school. I fought the likes of Mariano, Luis, Eric, Joseph, Edwin, Danny, Henry, Ecky, and a bunch of other nameless kids. I was very good at applying headlocks. I submitted a few enemies this way. I once scraped an opponent's face into the sidewalk, a nasty move I learned from my cousin Annie (RIP). Once I started getting serious about the martial arts and training more, I was able to avoid many of these types of scraps and altercations. I started avoiding certain environments that could lead to violence. My martial arts discipline became more prevalent. And my behavior improved as I had much more self-control. Yup!

97. Graffiti, 1984

In the summer of 1984, my cousins Sammy (RIP), Paulie, and myself used to go bombing. We tagged the inside of trains. Motion tagging. A group of other kids always joined us in our writing excursions on the greasy, grimy subway lines. We weren't kings or anything like that, just a bunch of juvenile delinquents hitting the layups. No burners, just tags. We hit the 4, 5, 6, and D lines—Maez one, Sect one, Welk one, Ork, Sam Ski (RIP), and several others. The whole crew included Paulie, Sammy (RIP), Carlos, Ismael, Jose, Simon, Alex, Robert, Ruben, and myself. We all resided on Decatur Avenue in the Bronx. All of us made our own markers. We racked up (stole) carbon ink paper from the school office that we attended at the time. We then filled a bucket with alcohol and dropped the ink paper in, letting it sit for a few days. The ink bled from the paper which we then used to fill our empty markers and shoe griffin bottles. We were ready for war.

We usually headed out to the subway station at about 11:00 p.m., the D train at 205th Street, or the 4 Train at Woodlawn Avenue.

I always thought, *Subway trains, here we come!* The rush was amazing. The fear of cops, thugs, criminals, psychopaths, maniacs, nut jobs, and other writers was intense. I always packed my nunchakus just in case. I yelled at my cousins, "Fuck that, somebody's head is getting busted wide open if they start some shit!" We all headed out to the trains in full force. We were about ten strong. It reminded me of the classic 1979 Paramount movie *The Warriors*, the opening scene where they board the train in Coney Island and head to the Bronx. We cracked jokes and ranked (mocked) on one another all the way to the subway station. Momma disses was our favorite pastime as we made our way to the train. These were a few of the gems that we dropped on one another: (1)"Your momma is so fat that when she stepped on the scale it said 'to be continued'!" (2) "Your momma is so fat that when she rolled over a dollar bill, she made change!" (3) "Your house is so dirty that even the roaches wear slippers!" (4) "Your momma is so old her social security number is number 2!" (5) "Your momma is so skinny she can dodge out raindrops!" We all cracked up with laughter. A bunch of teenagers just screwing around and having fun.

Sammy (RIP) always brought his radio boom box on all our journeys into the subterranean depths of the city. He tried to get a few us to carry it. Sammy (RIP) asked, "Yo, do me a favor and help me carry this."

"Hell no, not me!" I replied.

The boom box was very heavy. Nobody wanted to carry that shit, especially if we had to run from the cops or thugs. Once we reached the train station, we cased the place out. Looking out for five ohs (cops) or DTs(detectives). Undercover officers often hid behind a door with a small peephole. Sometimes, you could vaguely see an eyeball peering out from behind the peephole (there were no visible cameras on the subway back then), waiting for unsuspecting fare evaders to hop the turnstile. Many violators were caught and given summonses. Some were arrested. One of us (a scout) snuck past the front entrance gate, being very careful not to alert anyone. He alerted the rest of the crew if the coast was clear. Seeing that it was safe, all of us, one by one, hopped the turnstile or entered through the open gate. We entered slowly and cautiously, ready to take off if the fuzz (police) showed up.

All of a sudden, we were all startled when we suddenly heard a loud booming voice coming from the token booth. The clerk shouted at the top of his lungs over the PA system, "Pay your fare!" trying to alert any cops that might be nearby. "Shit, run!" we all shouted out loud, hauling ass as we took off like frightened rabbits. We gave the token booth clerk the middle finger as one of the guys in our crew simultaneously mooned him. We hustled down the ramp of the 205th Street D train station, trying to catch the arriving inbound train. The train roared into the station with burners and throw ups all over its side. We jumped onto the train, catching our breath after the wild ruckus. Hundreds of tags adorned the inside walls of the cars—EZ E, Menace Mel, Haz, Cope 2, Roach, Trap, Chino BYI, and countless others. We started ripping tags on the train as it started pulling out of the station. We were very careful not to go over other writers tags. That could most definitely start some beef or a fight. Trying to make more space, one of our guys brought a can of Coca-Cola and tried to acid burn some of the old tags off the walls left by other writers. Sometimes, we got off at the Bedford Avenue or Fordham Road stop. We tagged the station as quickly as possible but were very suspicious and wary of peering eyes.

For fun, we all played a game of chicken. It was more like a game of death. We all played by jumping off the subway platform and onto the tracks. You could see the train lights from the distance as it approached from the other station. The last person to climb back up from the tracks and onto the platform was declared the winner. I really loved this crazy game. It was totally demented and fucking nuts. Death-defying! Sammy (RIP) was overweight, so we had to hoist him back up onto the platform immediately. Some of the guys had nerves of steel and didn't flinch as the train slowly but surely made its way through the dark, ominous, and narrow tunnel toward our station. As the train got closer, you could clearly see the conductor in his booth maneuvering the massive steel-metal beast. That was enough for us. In a panicked frenzy, everyone started racing back up onto the platform. I always kept my calm. Somehow, I always felt I would be safe and nothing would go wrong. I was always the last one up—by choice, of course. I was declared the winner in the nick of time as the train roared into the station, and I felt the warm breeze it created as it danced across my back. I must've had a death wish. Yup. The D train stopped at 161st Street / Yankee Stadium. We hopped off the train and made our way through the popular subway stop. There was a police station inside the subway. We were very careful and did our best not to alert the cops. Remember, we all had markers and paint. I also had my nunchakus, and some of us had knives. My cousin Sam (RIP) always carried a butterfly knife.

On certain nights, we walked to the Gun Hill Road Station. It was located on the intersection of White Plains Road and Gun Hill Road. The 2 and 5 trains stopped there. We bombed that subway line too. We motion tagged being wary of undercover cops. The adrenaline rush was incredible. Sometimes we took the train to the Skate Key roller rink. We hung around, but we never went inside the iconic hangout. Other times we got off at Mosholu Parkway and ran amok around the neighborhood full of mischief. We always tried sneaking into an old dusty XXX-rated theater that was located right off the parkway. On one particular night, the whole crew was feeling rowdy and decided to toss a few discarded beer bottles into a bar full of patrons. We yelled as we opened the bar room door, and swoosh, the bottles made a loud crashing sound as they hit their mark. What the hell were we thinking! We were young and stupid. A pissed-off patron could've shot us. Everyone in our group started hauling ass. We ran as fast we could across Mosholu Parkway. Sammy (RIP) had the boom box and was struggling with it. He was on the portly side and couldn't run fast, so I gave him a hand with the radio as we made our escape. A bunch of crazy-ass kids. Yup!

Chapter 3 (1985–91)

98. Hot Dogs, 1985

In the beginning of 1985, Mom made the unruly decision to give her marriage one more shot. We soon packed up and left the Bronx. We ended up in Bridgeport once again. I wasn't a happy camper at this point. I was upset that I had no control of my life. My parents were extremely reckless in their behavior, and this totally ruined my ability to focus and do well in school. In 1984, I had attended five different schools in three different states. We resided in Bridgeport, Connecticut; Bronx, New York; Brooklyn, New York; and in Springfield, Massachusetts. We had a brief stint in Puerto Rico and New Haven, Connecticut, but I didn't attend school in those locations.

In 1985, Mom and I stood at a women's shelter based in New Haven, Connecticut. My brother, Edward, was living in a foster home elsewhere. My parents had separated at this point. It was after another major blowout. I spent most of my time wandering the neighborhood, twiddling my fingers and looking for some action. A Porsche dealer was nearby. Every day, for hours at a time, I gazed through the windows into the showroom. Porsche 911, 924, and 928—these cars were sleek and beautiful, and I vowed to one day own one, but if I wanted one, I had to first join the work force. My first real nine-to-five job was as a hot dog vendor. At the time, I was only fourteen years old. I got the job because my mom knew the owner of the company. I felt supercool working as a vendor. Finally, I had chance to make some real money. I was young but very responsible, or so I thought. The first day on the job was hectic. So on my first day to work, I was feeling cheery and whistling Dixie. When

I arrived to work, my new boss showed me the ropes. He taught me how to load the food cart with hot dogs, soda, napkins, straws, ketchup, mustard, relish, onions, and sauerkraut. He also explained the prices of all the items and how to make a swift sale. "Customer service is very important," he said. One more very important thing he taught me, and was very adamant about, was "to never open and start cooking new packs of hot dogs after lunchtime or noon." "Okay." I quickly blurted out.

The morning crowd was very slow. I sold a few cans of soda by 11:00 a.m., but not one hot dog. I thought, *This is a breeze, a piece of cake*. All of a sudden, a long line started massing in front of my cart. Construction workers, students, and people from all over the area gathered in front of me. "Holy stromboli," I whispered.

"Can I have a hot dog," one customer shouted, and then another customer and another, one after the next.

"Make mine with mustard please and hold the onions!" yelled yet another. "And don't forget the napkins."

It was a parade of several polite and a few rude customers as well. My head was about to explode. *Argh, what a nightmare!* I thought. It was like the classic film *Night of the Living Dead*. They kept coming and coming with no end in sight; my hands trembled nervously from the anxiety I felt. This was overwhelming, more than I anticipated. Finally, the rush was over.

After the initial onslaught, I looked into my cart and saw that there were only a few hot dogs left. I decided to throw a few unopened packs of hot dogs from the freezer into the cooker. About sixty hot dogs in all. About an hour later, it was extremely quiet. No customers at all. It was a ghost town. The time was 2:30 p.m. I looked into my cart. "The hot dogs are ready," I chirped. "What am I going to do?" So in a panic, I started eating them one by one. After about six or seven, I was stuffed. "Was I gonna be fired for my stupidity?" I gasped. At 4:30 p.m., I dragged my weary body and cart full of cooked unsold hot dogs back to the depot. The boss gave me a stern look and then chuckled, "Don't worry, buddy, first day mistake." Whew! Hot dog nightmare! Yup.

99. Moving to Brooklyn, 1985

Moving to East New York, Brooklyn, wasn't too bad for me, even though ENY was the murder capital of the United States at the time. Mom and I relocated to Brooklyn in the spring of May 1985. We shared an apartment with my cousin Nellie and my uncle Paul. We lived on Jamaica Avenue, in a small apartment on the second floor, right across the street from Highland Park. A kid named Manny and his two sisters lived on the first floor. I hung out with Manny sometimes. I made friends with some other local kids as well. I was a Bronx kid hanging with some Brooklyn kids. They were cool though.

Occasionally, I'd venture into Highland Park to work out on the playground. They had monkey bars, pull-up bars, and parallel bars. I felt like a kid in a candy store. I stretched, did calisthenics, and practiced my martial arts techniques. One day while training, I saw a guy doing pull-ups. He was extremely strong, muscular, and ripped. He looked like Steve Reeves from the classic *Hercules* movies of the '50s. This guy was chiseled. I wasn't a slouch myself. I worked out every day, but he was on another level. I slowly approached him, and he quickly turned and looked at me sternly. I guess he was being very wary and careful of strangers. After all, this was East New York, Brooklyn. I asked him about his daily training routine. I was a Bruce Lee fanatic myself, and this gentleman most assuredly had the definition and muscularity of the Little Dragon. He extended his hand out and humbly introduced himself as Billy. I thought, *This guy is supercool. Hopefully he'll train me.* I said, "I'm Anthony." Right then and there, he gave me a few pointers on exercise. He taught me how to break down sets and repetitions and showed me a wide variety of exercises on the apparatus. He put me on a training schedule. Every day thereafter, I trained under his wing. Speaking of wings, Billy had an incredible lat spread equal to Bruce Lee. I was like, "Shit, I want that too." Eventually, with his guidance, I got stronger and increased my muscularity. My lats expanded as well. I was able to do ten to fifteen pull-ups and dips per set. I felt really good. Billy did twenty-five reps per set for several sets. Soon after, I met Joe, who rocked (wore) a kung fu suit to the park. Joe was mad cool. He practiced a system called Wing Chun, the same style of kung fu that Bruce Lee learned from Yip Man. I was intrigued. I also met Mike (Billy's younger brother). He was twice as strong as Billy. Mike had the physique of the henchman Bolo from *Enter the Dragon*. He matched everything we did, but did it for fifty reps. This guy was totally unbelievable. We nicknamed him Popeye because of his massive forearms and triceps. He had a huge horseshoe of muscle forming his massive triceps. I, on the other hand, was known as Bruce Lee to the group due to my slender build and definition. To show off our well-earned physiques, we all wore white tank tops just like the one Bruce Lee donned in *Return of the Dragon*. I was in the park daily and trained from early in the morning to late in the evening. Other people jokingly referred to me as the statue in the park due to the fact that you could always find me there working out.

One afternoon, Joe and Mike were slap boxing in the park. It was an even match until Joe decided to use his Wing Chun maneuvers. Even though Mike was much stronger and extremely powerful, Joe was able to nullify his assault. Mike tried valiantly to get his punches through, but Joe shut him down rather easily and countered him every single time. They were friends and only playing around. Nevertheless, Joe dominated all the exchanges. Mike, not one to be outshined, scooped Joe up by both legs and gently slammed him into the ground. We all chuckled. I was very impressed by the Wing Chun that Joe had demonstrated in the park. I asked Joe, "Where did you learn that? Who taught you?"

He replied, "My boy Sifu Lenny."

"Can he teach me too?" I said.

"Sure, I'll ask him," Joe responded.

A few days later, I was at home and heard the doorbell ring. I went downstairs and saw Joe peering through the window of the door with a big Kool-Aid smile on his face. I opened the door and greeted Joe. A young Black gentleman with Jheri curls and a wide grin accompanied him. The gentleman smiled and said, "I'm Lenny, Lenny Mosley."

"Anthony," I greeted back.

147

Lenny was wearing a beautiful blue kung fu suit, the same one Bruce Lee wore in *Enter the Dragon*. Lenny asked me to demonstrate some kicks. I did some roundhouse and tornado kicks. Lenny did the first form in Wing Chun, Siu Nim Tao. He performed it flawlessly. We totally hit it off. We started meeting up several times a week after that for training. Lenny lived on Shepherd Avenue, about three blocks away on the second floor. On Sunday afternoons, a bunch of local martial arts guys from the neighborhood gathered at his home. We watched tons of kung fu movies—*Mystery of Chess Boxing, 7 Grandmasters, Drunken Master*, and all Jackie Chan films; *Hot Cool and the Vicious, The Marvelous Stunts of Kung Fu, The Flying Guillotine*, the *Five Deadly Venoms* films, *36th Chamber of Shaolin*, and all Gordon Liu films; Hwang Jang Lee films, Tan Tao Liang films; Billy Chong films; John Liu films; and of course, the Bruce Lee films, etc.

After a good dose of kung fu films, we all went down to the basement or front yard to get some physical practice. There were guys who trained in Shotokan, Wing Chun, boxing, Praying Mantis, taekwondo, jujitsu, Tiger claw, and street fighting, etc. Sparring matches were held with dudes getting rocked hard and knocked out cold. I had a match with a guy named Robert. He was bragging and talking nonsense about praying mantis kung fu and how useless it was. I had had enough of his antics. I said, "Okay, let's fight." It was the system I was practicing at the time. Lenny was the referee. Robert and I took neutral sides. As soon as Lenny said go, I quickly attacked and punched Robert in the face real hard with a right cross, knocking him out cold! It wasn't sparring for me, but a real fight. That was how I took it. Yup. Lenny had two brothers and a sister who lived on the first floor. His mom (RIP) lived with Lenny. We all kindly referred to her as Mrs. Davis. She was very sweet and gentle, but if you were rude and didn't have manners or show respect, then she'd most definitely give you a piece of her mind. She reminded me of my own mom. Lenny's older brother Lonnie didn't practice the martial arts whatsoever but ironically looked exactly like one of the villains in *Return of the Dragon"* We always laughed when the fight scenes came on with said character. Lenny's younger brother

Anthony (a.k.a. Mikey) was an avid martial artist. He loved wearing Bruce Lee tracksuits. You could catch him riding his motorbike around the neighborhood while flashing his *Game of Death* tights. Mikey was a real cool brother and had a great sense of humor. He always cracked jokes and lightened up the mood whenever necessary. Another martial artist I met back then was Kung Fu Derrick. His head was shaved like a Shaolin monk. He reminded me of the boxer Marvelous Marvin Hagler. Derrick was sort of rebel from society. He had tons of martial arts books and martial arts weapons. Derrick was a kind person, a true gentleman. When he visited my home, he always demonstrated good manners. My mom valued his good manners. Derrick trained in karate and kung fu and had his own following of martial arts students. He was a local legend in the neighborhood due to the fact that one evening, he was chased by cops on the elevated subway line for hopping the subway, and to evade capture, he leaped off the platform barefoot landing on the street below. The drop was about twenty feet. We remained friends for many years after, but unfortunately, Derrick's health began declining, and he was hit with financial hardship. Sadly, Derrick passed away soon after. RIP, Kung Fu Derrick.

There were many scrupulous figures in East New York in the 1980s. One person in particular was crazy Edwin. He was supposedly a kung fu master. He practiced the devil fist style. It was a concoction of his imagination and watching one too many kung fu movies. He walked around the neighborhood with a kung fu suit while challenging local martial artists. He usually got beat down. Edwin was in his thirties. Most of us were teenagers. One afternoon, a very young and sharp Taekwondo fighter named Jose (whom I first saw competing at the 1985 Ying Yee Kwoon championship in Brooklyn and winning the junior division that day) and I found ourselves in crazy Edwin's backyard. At first, everything was fine. Edwin gave us some refreshments, and then he invited us inside. We talked about Bruce Lee and martial arts. Suddenly, the conversation changed. Edwin wanted to practice Chi Sao (sticky hands). The Chi Sao quickly became a sparring match. Jose and Edwin went at it right in the middle of the living room with all his laundry strewn about the sofa. Jose got the best of him with his superior kicks. We all ended up back in the yard. Edwin decided to try his luck on me. I subdued him with some strikes. Finally, Edwin calmed down, caught his breath, and offered us a steak from the grill. Strange moment. Strange day. Yup. (Note: I actually first met Jose a few weeks after the Ying Yee Kwoon tournament. Ironically, we both attended Franklin K. Lane High School and began a conversation on the J train on our way home from school. I told him that I remembered him from the martial arts tournament. I told him I was training in the praying mantis kung fu style. We both got off at the Crescent Avenue station. We both demonstrated some moves. Jose did some great Taekwondo kicks. Jose was very flexible and a gifted athlete. I demonstrated some explosive tornado kicks and a form from the mantis style. We exchanged information and went our separate ways.)

I met Lenny in the summer of 1985. We were friends for thirty-five years. He always said "That's fresh!" with a big smile anytime he found something gracious or amusing. He truly loved the martial arts, comic books, great movies, and music. The New York Comic Con was one of his favorite endeavors that he attended every year. In his early years of hip-hop(1980s), he was known as the rapper Mystery MC. Lenny was a great person, father, husband, and was always there for everyone when they needed him. He worked for the NYPD school safety for over twenty years. Sadly, he passed away in 2020 from COVID-19. He left behind three sons. Many of my teenage years were spent with countless hours at his home. I'll miss you dearly, my friend. RIP, Kung Fu Lenny.

I was a big fan of the kung fu films that aired on TV throughout the '80s. Forty-Second street had a stretch of kung fu movie theaters across the avenue. It was only $2.99 for a three-film showcase. The theaters were tiny and filled with smoke, mostly from potheads smoking weed. I always hated the smell of marijuana. I felt it smelled like burnt horse crap. I didn't care though. I held my breath and sat there enjoying my kung fu flicks as best I could. I was astounded by all the acrobatic flips in the kung fu films and felt an immense need to do them myself. Years earlier, I practiced acrobatics with Barry Jefferson and Reginald Moore in Jersey City. I was able to do front flips, cartwheels, bridges, and monkey flips up to this point. Franklin K. Lane High School in Brooklyn, which I was attending at the time, had an afterschool gymnastics program. Actually, it was only a room filled with mats and apparatus (balance beam, pommel horse, high bar, vault, etc.). The so-called program was run by a bunch of students who were talented in flipping. There was no teacher. Everyone snuck in after the school dismissal bell rang. There were twin brothers who were very good at tumbling who practiced at the spot. They were so good that they would run to a wall and flip off it. They were amazingly talented. Several other kids who had some decent abilities practiced there as well. The guy who ran the practice was very cool. His name was Jose. He was a Dominican gentleman everyone called Flex. Many kids in the group were also into breaking (B-boying) and martial arts. Flex guided everyone on the fine points of tumbling. I had my monkey flips, but I really wanted to improve on my back hand springs. With Flex guiding me, I was able to develop my moves. "Keep your arms straight and lock your elbows and whip back as you quickly look for the floor!" he shouted out. One after one, all the dudes in the group kept trying to do the backflip, many landing on their heads, including myself. It was just like a scene right out of a Shaolin kung fu movie. In just two days, I was able to backflip cleanly. Every day after training, I went straight to Highland Park and practiced my flips on the baseball field. I did backflips around the bases. From first to second to third to home base, with all the sand and dust flying around from the wind. I was extremely determined to reach a higher level. The most continuous backflips I've done in a row were eleven. I was able to them like Reginald Moore traveling, but not like Barry Jefferson with the undercuts staying in one spot. Eventually, I learned to do aerial cartwheels, front, and back tucks as well. I must admit, I felt like one of the Five Deadly Venoms after learning to tumble, so well, thank you, Flex!

100. The Rumble, ENY, 1985

New York has always been known for its gang culture. East New York, Brooklyn, was a haven for gangs throughout the years.

The late '80s was notorious for drug posse. There were the infamous Hardy Boys, the Grant Street Boys, FFC (Fulton Fuck Up Crew), the Deceps, the Ballbusters, and others. Some of the members of these gangs hung out in Highland Park—Julio, Hulk, Baby Hulk, and Bee Ski just to name a few. They blasted their music on boom boxes, which I really enjoyed like classic hip-hop songs such as the "Inspector Gadget Rap" by Bad Boys or "La Di Da Di" by Dougie Fresh or Run-DMC's "Here We Go." I still had some of my breaking (breakdance) moves from the Bronx. I was itching to get down and bust out a few steps. One evening, while I was hanging out on the stoop of a building on Jamaica Avenue, I heard music blaring from the park. I saw a guy with a "Together We Chill" shirt throwing down. My friends and I started entering the park to join in the fun when suddenly gunshots rang out. Everyone scattered. *Damn!* I thought.

After that incident, I spent countless hours in the park, day in and day out. One day, the same gentlemen who played their boom boxes while hanging out suddenly swarmed and rushed toward a hill. I heard them yell out "Bushwick" as they charged forward. Some dudes from the Bushwick area were trying to start a scuffle with the East New York guys, which they quickly took care off. They were about twelve or more of them. They all disappeared into the forest adjoining the hill. A few moments later, they all returned and sat down on the park bench, proceeded to play music, and guzzled down on a few forty-ounce beers as well. I never had issues with them. My friend Fat Chris's older brother was down with them. These guys, or gang members if you would, protect the park so to speak. No one dared to start any problems with any of the gentlemen, that was until one evening.

Me and a few of my homeboys were playing a game of basketball in the park. We played around the world. It was Ronnie and his brother Mike, fat and skinny Chris, and a few other guys. We usually played basketball toward the evening hours when it wasn't so hot. We were doing our usual thing, enjoying ourselves over a game. We noticed that some guys were gathering nearby. Two groups were forming. On one side were members of the FFC, which were about eight to nine guys. On the other side were several guys from another area, including one muscular dude from a nearby YMCA gym. Beefs that night were going to be settled with a fair fight, one guy against one guy. We all moved up for a closer look, but not too close. There was a popular saying back then: "Bullets have no names." The scene that was unfolding before my eyes reminded me of the *West Side Story* or *Beat Street* where all the dudes stood on opposite sides of one another ready to do battle.

The fight started quickly. The leaders of both groups stepped forward and started letting their hands fly. At first, the smaller guy from FFC caught the muscular guy with several unanswered punches. The bigger fighter stepped up his game and began raining down punches on the smaller dude. The FFC fighter, not one to be outshined, scooped up the musclebound gentleman by his legs and body slammed him into the hard pavement. That was when the shit hit the fan. One of the musclebound guy's friends tried to separate them, and that was when one of the other dudes from FFC who was drinking a carton of orange juice smashed it into his face. The quart-sized carton exploded upon impact with juice being hurled all over the place. Rumble! Everyone from both sides jumped in and started swinging for the fences. Fists were flying all over the place. Dudes got punched, kicked, elbowed, slammed, and stomped. Miraculously, no guns or knives were drawn. There were more guys on the FFC side, so they definitely had the major advantage. About three or four FFC members pummeled the musclebound guy sense-less. The bloodied poor guy fell into the middle of the street on Jamaica Avenue blocking all traffic on both lanes with annoyed drivers trying to get to their destinations blowing their horns erratically. As the poor gentleman lay on the street in a pool of blood, the FFC dudes kicked him in the face and stomped his head mercilessly into the pavement. I remember guys wearing shell-topped Adidas and Pumas with fat laces joining in on the action. The musclebound guy's face was unrecognizable. His friends who were battle worn from the rumble scooped him up and carried him off into the dark-ness to the emergency room at the hospital perhaps. The FFC guys dusted themselves off and returned to the park bench to chill out. All was normal again. We, on the other hand, continued to finish our basketball game. Swoosh! Yup!

101. Long Arm of the Law, 1985

I was hanging out one night on the corner of Jamaica Avenue and Elton Street in East New York. It was a hot summer night, and kids were playing everywhere. Families were gathered in front of their homes, relaxing or playing cards or dominoes. Little girls played hopscotch or double Dutch while young boys played tag or some other sort of street games. I chilled (relaxed) with a few friends on the corner, cracking jokes.

The beautiful evening calm was about to end. From a distance of about a half mile, a ruckus was taking place. Police lights could be seen from afar, but no sound could be heard yet. My friends and I started watching more intently. It looked like a car chase from a 1970s cop show. The cars were getting closer to where we were all gathered at. Several police cruisers were engaged in the hot pursuit of a runaway car. They crossed Pitkin, Liberty, and then Atlantic Avenue. We could now hear the sirens blaring as they were almost upon us. There were many bumps and potholes on the road, which caused the cars to screech and bounce up and down with sparks flying everywhere. Parents quickly grabbed their children in a hurried attempt to escape the insanity. People ran in all directions to avoid the onslaught. The runaway car zoomed down the street at breathtaking speed with the cops right on his tail, and then with a loud crashing boom, the car crashed into another civilian car. It wasn't over yet as the criminal jumped out of the mangled wreckage and tried to make a run for it. A large, hulking officer emerged from one of the police vehicles. He must have been about six foot, five inches easily. The officer was quick on his feet though, as he continued to pursue the criminal on foot. The giant cop caught up to the man and grabbed him by his shirt, scooped him up into the air with one arm, and then slammed him thoroughly into the ground. The man was out like a light as the cop quickly handcuffed him and threw him in the back of the cruiser. The officer resembled the wrestling champion Hulk Hogan. One for the good guys. Thank God no one was hurt. Yup.

102. Sensei Gooden, PAL, 1985

Once I moved to Brooklyn, I trained with several great teachers. Sensei Gooden at the local Police Athletic League located on Pennsylvania Avenue in East New York taught me the ins and outs of grappling. He taught jujitsu. He was an older Black gentleman with gray hair. He was very nice but very stern. He was short with a medium build and walked with a slight limp. His hands were very strong, and he had really thick fingers. When he grabbed me in his vice grip and put me into a wrist lock or choke hold, the pain was so intense I swear I saw the Virgin Mary appear. There was absolutely no talking in class unless it was the senpai (seniors) giving out instructions. If sensei caught you talking, he'd limp across the mats to where you were standing and use you as an uke (partner). He would then demonstrate the effectiveness and usefulness of jujitsu, and boy, was it effective. Students in the class stayed very focused and didn't want to slip up and become the shining example of sensei's behavior modification jujitsu techniques. We all stood on our toes so to speak. Kids at PAL used to peer through the door window of the class and watch what was unfolding. Most kept their distance. Sensei was a hardened old-school, no-nonsense type of instructor. The kids all knew it. The real students trained hard, never losing sight of that fact.

Once in a while, someone would stroll into class and try to disrupt the flow of the of the training, but rest assured, sensei would always set things straight. My friend Skinny Chris was one such person. Chris was a jokester. He was a really funny guy. But the dojo was no standup comedy room. One night, he decided to attend a free class tryout. When he arrived, he quickly tried making everyone in the class crack up with his funny-man antics. The class just watched him, but no one laughed. They knew what was about to happen. Sensei's office door swung wide open, and he then proceeded to limp across the floor as was his usual routine. All eyes opened wide as Chris kept yapping away, unaware of what was about to take place.

Everyone moved off to the side to make space for sensei. Chris kept going on and on with his jolly laughter. Sensei tapped him on the shoulder. Sensei said, "You can be my uke!"

"What's an uke?" Chris replied.

"Let me show you," replied sensei.

Chris went flying up in the air as sensei demonstrated a wide array of jujitsu movements. The laughter was gone. Everyone in the class grimaced at the agony Chris was now facing. Sensei demonstrated one lock after another and finally finished it off with a choke hold. The wide smile Chris shared with the class was now a thing of the past. That was a hard lesson learned. Chris never returned, like so many others. Martial arts was serious business. Eventually, Sensei Gooden packed up and moved to California. Other instructors came in to teach, but it just wasn't the same. Yup!

103. Dragon Claw Institute, 1985–87

After ending up in Brooklyn, I spent many hours watching kung fu films and practicing whatever martial skills I had up to that point. Mom and I decided to drive around, looking for a new school. She had a new job and wanted me to continue the martial arts I so dearly loved. We drove around to a few different schools, but none of them left an impression on me. As we headed back home, I noticed a sign that read "Dragon Claw Institute." I said, "Mom, stop here!" She slowed down and parked the car. I quickly jumped out of the car with Mom behind me. As I approached the sign, I realized that it was a kung fu school. I looked through the window and saw some commotion inside. We walked in and were greeted by a very nice gentleman. He gave us some basic information and said, "You can sit here and watch." The school looked like a scene right out of the martial arts movies I loved watching. The students practiced some exotic-looking kung fu moves. Mom said, "These people are dancing." But I knew, or at least had an idea, of what they were doing. I knew then and there that I wanted to join the school. Mom was like, "Are you sure?" and I replied, "Yes, I'm very sure!" Mom signed me up. They gave me some kung fu pants with a very cool T-shirt with the membership. I was very ecstatic and looking forward to my first class.

I arrived for my initial day of training with a lot of enthusiasm. I wore a pair of chinese slippers with my outfit. There were a few guys in the class—my seniors in mantis-style kung fu which included Steve, Ricky, Milton, Luis, Christian, Irving, Raymond, Hector Jr, and several others. The *sigong* (master) of the school was George Ruiz. He was very stern and serious about practice. He was very strong and fit. He drilled us in traditional Chinese kung fu. We did tons of push-ups, ab exercises, deep stretching, leaps and jumps, running, low-stance training, forms, weapons, two-man drills, and free sparring. I really loved the training. It was at times very harsh and demanding, which gave us wonderful results. We were a very sharp and competitive group. Some of the best guys in our school were top-notch competitors who traveled from tournament to tournament on the east coast. They won many competitions.

One morning, we all woke up at four o'clock and hopped on a van owned by Hector Jr.'s dad. He was the owner of the building (school) as well. It was a long, bumpy ride. The tournament was called Anthony Goh's Kung Fu Championship, which was held in Baltimore, Maryland. It was about a four- or five-hour drive from New York. We listened to the radio most of the way. Starship's "We Built This City" was a top hit on the airwaves at that time. We sang that tune at the top of our lungs. Some of the guys, including myself, dozed off in the back from lack of sleep. When we arrived at the tournament, the guys quickly registered and competed in their assigned rings. It was a good day for the school as the guys did well and placed respectively in their divisions. Sihing Ricky competed in forms; Sihing Hector Jr. competed in empty hands and weapons; Sihing Raymond competed in forms, broad sword, spear and chain whip; Sihing Irving competed in spear and chain whip; Sihing Luis competed in double hook swords; Sifu Christian competed in kumite; and Sifu Steve competed in forms. After the tournament, we stopped at a local McDonalds and got a few burgers. We slept for most of the ride home after. The guys took a few days off after the tournament, then it was back to the *kwoon* (school).

We trained during the cold of winter and the hot, humid summer. There was no heat in the school due to the fact that there was no boiler. It was corroded to the core. To stay warm, we had to train hard and elevate our body temperature. Smoke could be seen rising from our bodies through our sweat-soaked T-shirts. In the summer months, it was grueling. There was no air conditioner to cool us down. There were no water breaks as well. As a matter of fact, I never saw water bottles like we see prevalent today. It was balls-to-the-wall training. Forms and weapons practice was great. Guys leaping about the school performing dazzling and eye-catching acrobatic moves. Sparring was very tough. We did arm slapping drills with traditional kung fu blocks. Everyone's arms were red with welts and bruises. We trained leg-sweep kicks and maneuvers as well. Guys got swept hard and took a lot of falls. I got swept once or twice myself. I also swept a few guys down in the process as well. I had many black-and-blue marks on my shins from the constant hard impact. They were my scars of love.

Sifu Christian was a real badass. He was relentless in sparring and had powerful kicks and strikes. He unleashed his fury on all of us underlings. I trained really hard just so that I could spar with him. I ran at 4:00 a.m. every day. I remember going to the park for an early run and thinking "I'm the first one here!" and then suddenly seeing an old man swoosh by me and lap me. He was slick as a whistle. I was rather annoyed, you might say. To boost my strength, every day at the break of dawn, I drank several raw eggs just like Rocky. And I did tons of conditioning drills. I skipped rope every morning as well, with the music blaring in the background. Mom wasn't too happy about that. When Sifu Christian and I sparred, I was able to hold my own. I was a very strong kid and had no fear for fighting, but I must say, Sifu Christian helped me become a much better fighter. He kicked like a mule, especially when he whipped those back leg roundhouse kicks. *Oh boy, lookout!* I thought to myself *Here it comes!* He was the real deal and tough as nails.

Eventually, sigong decided to go to the Armed Forces, and the school didn't survive for long after that. It was a sad time. The training I received at Dragon Claw Institute was incredible, and I would still teach some of their methods to my students today. Thank you, Sigong George Ruiz!

104. Tommy Chen

I was referred to Shihan Tommy Chen by Shihan Jonas Nunez in the Bronx. Jonas was a great teacher and had a beautiful dojo he shared with Sensei Douglas Tsoi. The dojo was located near Bedford Park, a few blocks from the 4 Train and D train subway stop. Shihan Jonas gave some great classes with tons of flexibility work and conditioning drills. He also had the basement full of free weights and stretching machines for the students to use. Shihan Jonas also had a little room in the back where he lived, and it had a TV and refrigerator. I was very inspired by his setup. I said to myself, "Hmm, I could do this." I spent some quality time training with Jonas, but the trip to the Bronx from Brooklyn was excruciatingly long. Jonas said, "You should go train with my teacher, Shihan Tommy Chen. He's much closer to you." Shihan Tommy was in Brooklyn and much easier to get to. His dojo was located on Avenue H. It was near Brooklyn College.

The first time I stepped foot into his dojo, I was seventeen. I had trained for a couple of years up to that point. He reminded me of one of the characters from Channel 5's the *Ten Tigers of Kwangtung* kung fu movie. As I entered the dojo, he slowly exited from his office and looked at me up and down. Shihan Tommy Chen was soft spoken and very polite. I actually had called him over the phone earlier explaining my dilemma. He then proceeded to ask me several questions. Afterward, he said, "Now show me what you can do." I did some splits, tornado kicks, and high side kicks. He said, "Very good!" I became a member of the dojo and traveled day in and day out to practice. The ride was about one hour, but much shorter than the two-hours-plus ride to the Bronx.

I received a KI-brand blue karate uniform. I trained several nights a week, including on the weekends. I basically lived there. I came in at 4:30 p.m. and left at 11:30 p.m. The training was great. Shihan was very skilled at weaponry and taught me several. I had a few classmates including Chris, Mac, Desmond, Edwin, Paul, and several others. Some nights were sparring nights as everyone geared up. On other nights, we practiced acrobatics and aerial moves, and on some nights, kata and self-defense. Shihan was very patient, as most of us were teenagers and had very little understanding of certain things. I helped him occasionally with some classes and helped give out flyers and tidy the dojo. I started competing in martial arts tournaments more frequently under his guidance. I had some success but still had much to learn. On some evenings, shihan and a few of the guys would hang around the dojo after hours, chatting it up and sharing a few jokes and stories. We always ordered Chinese food from the next-door restaurant as we sat together. It was a fun time. We also watched martial arts videos and sporting events like the 1988 Olympic games. We watched the taekwondo matches on channel 4, NBC. The American team's Jay Warwick was dismantled by his Korean opponent for the gold medal.

I eventually tested and received my black belt from Shihan Tommy Chen in December of 1989. I was elated, as it was one of the happiest moments of my life. I eventually branched out to open several dojos of my own. Thank you, shihan, for your lessons and guidance through the years. Osu!

105. Holy Intervention, Chess, 1985

One Sunday morning my uncle Paul and I were having breakfast. We lived on a second-floor apartment with my mom and my cousin Nelly in Brooklyn. We were having some clever conversation over coffee and a sandwich. My uncle shared his morning paper with me. I read the Sunday comics. *Hagar the Horrible, Broom Hilda, Garfield, Peanuts,* and *Calvin and Hobbes* were among several of my favorites. My uncle read his usual sports section.

After breakfast, we started cleaning up the kitchen. There was a loud thunderstorm outside. The rain was coming down hard. My uncle was washing dishes. I was tidying up the table and was about to discard the morning paper when I noticed an intriguing article. It mentioned something about the Dead Sea Scrolls. I briefly looked over the article. It said that some missing parts to the old Bible were recently discovered in the Black Sea, and it also mentioned a connection to the end of times. I showed it to my uncle. He was very skeptical about the whole thing and said, "They've been talking about the end of the world for a long time. It's all nonsense!" At the same instance, a loud crack of thunder could be heard right next to our kitchen window, and a bluish lightning bolt came right through it and passed between where my uncle and I were standing. The bolt raced toward the ceiling and entered through the light fixture. *Kaboom!* It was a deafening sound. I was frozen in place. My uncle stood motionless near the sink in shock. We looked at each other. I told him, "Never make fun of God again!" He agreed.

Several weeks later, my uncle relocated to the Bronx with my cousin Nelly. I was seventeen at the time. One morning, my uncle and I decided to go for a long run in Van Cortlandt Park, which was located nearby and was widely known for holding citywide track meets. We ran Cemetery Hill. It had a steep incline and lots of other wavy hills. I was an avid runner by this time, as I was doing roadwork in Highland Park in Brooklyn on a daily basis. My uncle was a runner since he was a teen. Always competitive, we both sped through the hills and flats until we finished our run. I finished my run ahead of my uncle. He said, "Very good." When we got back home, my uncle started making a pot of coffee and suggested a game of chess. We always played chess for fun. I never beat my uncle once in the eleven years that we had partaken in the activity. But something was different that day. I felt elated from the great run. My uncle said, "Would you like some carrot cake with your coffee?"

I responded with a resounding "Yes, thank you!" I really loved coffee with carrot cake. We both sat down at that table for our snacks over a game.

My uncle said, "You're white, the challenger. You go first."

I said, "Okay." I played the white side for more than half my life, and I was rather used to it. "Yummy, this cake is delicious!" I said as I took a few bites.

My uncle said, "Make your move." I played my first piece. He then moved his pawn. The game was on. I was more focused on my cake than on the game, so I hastily ate it. Now I was focused on the board in front of me. My uncle's focused was laser like. I said to myself, "Hmm, I've got to concentrate."

We were about ten minutes into the game, and I was able to take his queen. My uncle was irate. He shifted his attack to his castles/rooks. I noticed things in the game that I hadn't before. I saw flaws in his defense and quickly counterattacked his advances. He was now at my mercy. He tried valiantly to survive, but surprisingly, I had the upper hand. I saw the moment I had been waiting for eleven years and slammed my piece on the board and yelled out, "Checkmate!" He couldn't believe it. My uncle was livid and said, "Let's play again!" But again, I was victorious, and then again, I beat him three times in a row that day. My time had come. He got up left the table and turned on the TV and proceeded to watch a game of basketball. Sorry, Uncle Paul. Yup!

106. Domestic Violence, Upstairs, 1985

I was no stranger to domestic violence growing up. I saw my fair share of family skirmishes. Mom separated and left Dad when I was fifteen. We relocated to Brooklyn in 1985 to start a new life. It was a breath of fresh air. Finally, peace and quiet and no more squabbles. I had to do my best to adjust to the slower-paced lifestyle. Mom started working as a cashier at Western Beef Supermarket. She also started attending York College and then Boricua College. She worked long, tiresome hours and studied endlessly. By the time she got home, she was totally worn-out. She'd make dinner if she was able to muster up enough energy. It wasn't easy for her, but she was courageous and met every challenge head on.

After many years of long sacrifice, she finally earned a degree in social work. She was awarded this honor at Saint Patrick's Cathedral in New York, alongside many other recipients. I must say, I felt a deep sense of overwhelming pride. Mom had faced so much adversity in her life but was able to overcome them. She was a strong woman whose unbending faith in God pushed her to new heights. Mom looked beautiful in her gown and cap. When she walked down the aisle to receive her diploma, I felt so happy. She smiled from ear to ear. Well-deserved. I love you, Mom.

As a teen, I had to learn how to do several things for myself. Mom was extremely busy with work and school, so I had to step it up. I was always hungry and ravaged the refrigerator. My appetite had increased tenfold as a teen and also due to the fact that I was always working out. Sure, I knew how to cook a few things like scrambled eggs, a burger, pancakes, etc., but I wanted to cook some of the dishes Mom used to make. So I experimented in the kitchen. I tried my hand at cooking rice, potatoes, steak, chicken, pasta, and other foods. In the beginning, I nearly burned down the house. Smoke filled the apartment from overcooked meals. The fire alarms constantly went off as my poor neighbors upstairs could be heard running around their apartments in a panic. Gradually, my cooking improved. I'd cook for Mom sometimes. A hot meal would be waiting for her when she got home. I knew she really appreciated it.

Mom had a friend named Elizabeth who lived upstairs. She was a very nice lady and had two sons and two daughters—Joey, Jose (Puchy), Jennifer, and Lisa. Mom and her spent a lot of time talking about life. I always hung out with Puchy playing video games, cards, and practicing karate. I had two cats during this time named Fiffy and Spooky and a dog named Gizzy. Puchy would always bring my cats back home every time they ventured off. His little sister Jennifer liked playing with Gizzy. One evening while I was home with Mom watching TV, a loud commotion startled us. Elizabeth ran downstairs holding her nose. There was blood everywhere. She was attacked. She cried to my mom for help. I quickly grabbed my nunchaku sticks. I was ready to crack someone over the head. I ran to the door and bolted it. Elizabeth said that her estranged husband came by and got angry and assaulted her. I was furious. Mom had gone through things like that before. Mom cleaned her up and calmed her down. Elizabeth said she didn't want her kids to see her like that, especially her oldest son Joey, who just might lose it. I believed the youngest child, Jennifer, who was in tears witnessed the attack. I grabbed a mop and Clorox and thoroughly cleaned up the blood on the stairs and floor.

A few days later, I saw Elizabeth's husband in front of the house. Everything was calm as it seemed that they got back together. Strange. Yup.

107. Devil Worshippers, Brujería, Highland Park, 1985

Ever since I was a kid, I constantly heard about *brujería* (witchcraft). It was part of our Puerto Rican folklore that dated back to Spain and Africa. Heck, there was even a song written on the topic from a well-known salsa band called El Gran Combo. As a child, I had many nightmares due to the overindulgence to horror films. I watched a lot of movies about the topic, so I did my best to steer clear of such things. I was raised in a religious household, and I prayed every night before going to bed. Mom always recited Psalm 23 from the Bible with me—"The Lord is my shepherd. I shall not want." We also always made sure to say *bendición* to our parents and our loved ones. They always responded by saying "Que Dios te bendiga." The meaning behind *bendición* was "asking for their blessing." "Que Dios te bendiga" meant "May God bless you." I always slept better at night after blessings.

Years later, I found myself running early in the mornings in Highland Park in East New York, Brooklyn. I ran up and down the hills and across the fields and pavement. There was a trail that ran around a defunct aqueduct, which was over a mile long. I usually did three laps for endurance. It was an obstacle course of dead animals. Chickens, cats, dogs, rodents, and rabbits adorned the trail. These animals did not die by natural causes. They were killed as a ritual sacrifice for witchcraft. People were afraid to go up there. Only weirdos and die-hard runners were brave or foolish enough to do so. I didn't give a hoot. I had to train just like Rocky. So I ventured courageously into the area. I ran at top speed as I hurdled over all the dead carcasses to avoid encountering any spells or misfortune. I was fast as the wind due to the motivating factors involved. Yup.

108. Murders NYC

The crime rates in New York City were ridiculous in the 1970s and 1980s. Murders, rapes, robberies, assaults, burglaries, prostitution, and drug dealing were on the rise. The New York mob ran things from the top. Gangs and drug posse ruled the streets. I remember a few such notorious groups: The Hardy Boys, Fulton Fuck Up Crew (FFC), Together We Chill, Decepticons (Deceps), the Ballbusters (Dominicans), the Lowlife Crew, Money…Sex…and Drugs (MSD), Jamaican Posse, etc.

I've witnessed many beatdowns on the LL subway train at the Broadway Junction / East New York station. (Ironically, it was the same station where *The Warriors*, a 1979 movie about a street gang from Coney Island, was filmed.) The Decepticons ran amok at Broadway Junction. It was their turf. There was a police station at the bottom of the station, but nevertheless, the Deceps terrorized the subways riders on the upper half of the station as they pulled into the stop. Groups of about twenty to twenty-five young teens pummeled and assaulted innocent victims daily. It was called wilding. I once saw a young guy get surrounded on the train as the gang pounced on him and stomped him out. It was crazy! On the JJ train, which pulled into the same station, it was no better. Young women's gold hoop earrings were being snatched off in plain daylight. Blood splattered everywhere. It was total carnage. The ladies cried holding their mangled and mutilated earlobes. I was totally disgusted. People, including myself, wanted to intervene, but there were just too many Deceps in numbers.

The trains were a battleground, and the city was in a war—a war against crime. Always be on the alert! Never let your guard down. The streets were worse than the trains. Dark alleys, broken street lights, drug dealers on every corner, crackheads looking for their next hit, stick-up kids (armed robbers) on the prowl, etc. Man, be alert! This shit is real! Yup!

109. Murder 1, East NY, Summer 1985

I witnessed my first homicide in East New York, Brooklyn, in 1985. East New York and adjoining Cypress Hills were the murder capital of the United States at that time. This act of violence sadly took place on the corner of Linwood Street and Ridgewood Avenue on a very hot and humid summer night in the city. I had seen death before—old woman hit by a car, at wakes in funeral homes, and mostly in the movies and on TV, but this was a real murder, a savage act of cowardice. A soul that was ripped from the body. A life that unfortunately ended too short at the hands of another human being.

The young man tragically killed on that evening was only fifteen years old. I was the same age as the victim at the time. Up till then, I could never conceive of a fifteen-year-old being murdered, but age was irrelevant. These harsh streets took no prisoners. I was home on this night and heard a loud commotion outside. I saw lights and heard police car sirens and NYPD helicopters buzzing overhead. There were many people gathered on the corner with police tape blocking them off. I joined the crowd. *What's this? Must be an accident*, I thought. There was something on the street. I moved closer for a better look. There was hump, something underneath a blanket. I asked myself, "What is that? A dog perhaps." I decided to ask several bystanders that were standing nearby some questions; everyone was mum. No one spoke a word. I worked my way around the police tape. DTs (detectives) were everywhere with their flashlights, pens, and notepads, jotting down notes. I thought for a moment, *All this for a dog? I don't think so!*

Finally, I ran into my friend Jason. He lived on the corner. "Yo, what happened?" I asked him.

"Someone got killed," he immediately responded. I quickly assumed it must've been a car accident. I surely thought this must be the case. I asked Jason, and he said, "No, he was beat up with a baseball bat and then shot to death." Reality check 101. I've never seen anyone murdered before. I've seen beatdowns and robberies, but never a homicide. My dad had guns, but never fired one in my presence. This was very new for me. Scary! *But why, how can anyone ever kill someone and for what? How is this possible?* I pondered. I recalled John Lennon being shot and killed and President Ronald Reagan getting shot on live TV. But tonight, this was very different; it took place in my own backyard, in my own neighborhood. "Who was the culprit, the killer?" I worried. I looked at all the faces in the crowd with utter suspicion. If they could kill him, they could kill me. I became paranoid. I was always on the streets playing my boom box, breaking, and practicing my martial arts. Now, I had to be wary of every stranger, keep my guard up, watch my back, and constantly look over my shoulder. Damn, this sucked! Jason told me how things went down. He said, "Supposedly, the victim made some remarks to a girl who was walking by. She was the girlfriend of a local gang leader. The thugs returned soon after and confronted the victim. Words were exchanged. The bats came out and the pistols too. He was killed in front of his home while his mom was inside the house."

I told Jason, "This shit is crazy. Just for that! These bastards will kill you for anything."

That night, something in me drastically changed. I knew then and there that evil existed.

The body was on the street for some time. Finally, after a long wait, the coroner had arrived. Detectives collected bullet casings and fragments from the crime scene, gathering as much evidence as possible. The coroner, on the other hand, took several pictures of the young victim from different angles. Everyone in the crowd gasped as the entry and exit wounds from the gunshots became apparent. Sadly, a few minutes later, the victim's older brother arrived home. He was in his early twenties. He had a Jheri curl hairstyle and was wearing a black Michael Jackson zipper jacket. He was Latino, Puerto Rican perhaps. The gentleman walked up to the police tape with a puzzled look on his face. He attempted to cross the line but was stopped by the cops. They spoke to him. You could just barely make out the conversation between them. The gentleman said he lived in the home. He yelled out in frustration, "What's going on?" The detectives escorted him toward the sheet-covered corpse. The officers wanted to identify who was underneath. Maybe the victim was a local drug dealer or thug or some other acquaintance. I'll never forget what happened next. They removed the sheet. I'm almost in tears as I wrote this down. The man let out the most piercing scream. It penetrated my soul, my very existence. Everyone present became silent. No one spoke or uttered a word out of respect. The detectives lowered their heads. The man wailed in tears over the body, crying violently, unfathered by shame. It was his little brother. This was unbearable for me. I had an older brother. We were inseparable growing up. I loved him to death, still do. My god, this was horrible! East New York. Yup.

110. Murder 2, East NY, Summer 1985

On this sweltering summer night, Kung Fu Derrick, Joe English, and I walked around our Brooklyn (East New York) neighborhood. We spoke about martial arts and other topics as well. Joe always carried his boom box radio, playing all the radio hits and mix tape cassettes too. After strolling the area for some time, the three of us decided to get some heartwarming pizza. Caterinas Pizzeria on Fulton Street and Elton Street was the best spot around. The owners were Sal and Vito. Two very nice Italian gentlemen. Everything at Caterinas was delicious. The slices were huge with drippy cheese and sauce. Everyone in the neighborhood loved this place. (Amazingly, the pizzeria is still standing today after more than forty years.) After stuffing our faces, we headed out. We walked underneath the elevated J train subway line. We passed Norwood Avenue, which was an extremely notorious area for drug pushing. Crack was wreaking havoc on the streets during this time. We walked and talked till we reached Fulton Street and Crescent Avenue.

Derrick wanted to visit a local martial arts school nearby. It was called Yoo Dan Ja's Taekwondo, a really tough local Korean martial arts school (dojang). I noticed a very talented young martial artist named Jose Nunez, who was a student there. He had great kicks and was extremely flexible. I first saw him competing at a tournament called Ying Yee Kwoon in Brooklyn the same year. Jose won the junior advanced divisions in fighting and kata. Derrick knew a gentleman named Trent, who also trained at the school. They had a few parting words, and then the three of us decided to head back home. It was a long walk back. Joe blasted his boom box. As we approached the Norwood Avenue train station, we could see lights blaring in the distance. Joe turned off the radio. As we got bit closer, the police tape became visible as the crime scene of the shooting victim was now apparent. Cops were everywhere. The officers methodically investigated and probed the area, searching for evidence to the rhyme or reason for the heinous act. The poor victim who was Caucasian with blond hair was shot numerous times including the face, stomach, and armpit. The victim was shirtless, which made his wounds easy to see. We departed after a few minutes, and all went home. Another night in Brooklyn, East New York. Yup.

111. Murder 3, East NY, Summer 1985

I used to hang out at a poolroom that was located on the corner of Linwood Street and Fulton Avenue. It was underneath the J train elevated platform. It was known as a drug spot. I went there for one reason and one reason only: video games. They had two games that I really enjoyed: Kung Fu Master and Yie Ar Kung Fu. All the local kids gathered there to play a few rounds daily. I was no different. One night, I found myself playing there at about 10:00 p.m., swishing, swirling, kicking, and fighting with all sorts of weapons. Yie Ar Kung Fu was a very cool game that had Shaolin monks as the main characters. So I guess, I found this game rather intriguing due to the fact that I was training at a local kung fu school called Dragon Claw Institute. It was located near the Van Siclen Avenue train stop. The training consisted of praying-mantis style kung fu and wushu. Weapons training was also a very integral part of the class.

So anyway, here I was, late at night in the video room playing video games when suddenly, some bright lights from the sidewalk came on. It was a huge police strobe light, exactly like the one in the *Batman* cartoons that highlighted the bat insignia in the nighttime sky. It lit up the whole area, including the game room. (Fulton Street was really dark back then due to drug dealers shooting out the street lights. In this way, they were able to run their illegal narcotics businesses unnoticed. This made it much easier for them to peddle their wares, crack/cocaine, to the poor souls who were entrenched by their evil grasp.) I quickly stopped playing my game and looked outside to see what was going on, so I was like, "Yo, what the hell is going on!" I stepped outside to see what was up. I assumed it must've been a drug raid. The usual cops and detectives were on hand investigating the situation. *This was no drug bust!* I thought to myself. The police set up a perimeter with tape around the crime scene rather quickly. Some black garbage bags were strewn about the sidewalk. The detectives pricked and pried the bags. They slowly opened them one by one only to reveal multiple body parts inside. Someone got hacked and slashed and chopped into itty-bitty pieces. Surreal. Probably a drug deal gone bad. The officers took several pictures of the scene. I was kind of getting used to seeing these types of things by then. Detectives must've surely put in a lot of overtime in the 1980s. Anyway, I went back and resumed playing my video game. Another night in East New York, 1980s. Yup!

112. Murder 4, East NY, Summer 1986

One evening, a few friends and I were outside playing football. It was a bunch of guys from the block, including some of the following: Ronnie, Mike, Skinny Chris, Fat Chris, Nick, Marlon, Sebastian, Marcos, Jason, Henry, and Richie. On that night, we decided to play on the corner of Cleveland Street and Jamaica Avenue, right across the street from Highland Park. It was late in the evening, but that never stopped us before. So here we were, tossing the ball back and forth, short pass, long pass! "Go deep!" the quarterback yelled out to the wide receivers. We had a lot of fun roughhousing one another for the sake of sport.

On one of the miscalculated throws, the ball accidently hit a car's windshield really hard, almost shattering it. I ran up to the car to retrieve the ball. I checked to see if the windshield was cracked. I hoped it wasn't. We were all broke and didn't have money to fix it. To my dismay, as I peered into the vehicle, I saw someone sleeping inside. He was on the passenger side with his feet suspended in air. He looked very familiar. "Hmm who is that?" I said faintly. The other guys ran up as well to take a look inside. "Is he asleep?" someone blurted out. "Maybe he's drunk!" someone else shouted out loud. I knocked on the window softly at first, then louder, but he didn't respond.

Upon closer inspection, we saw a trickle of blood running from his temple to his cheekbone. There was a small hole—a gunshot wound! I finally recognized the victim. It was the front clerk from the local bodega (deli). It was located on Elton Street and Ridgewood Avenue. *Crazy, what a damn shame! He was such a nice guy*, I thought. He used to always let me slide whenever I was short a few cents for a bag of chips, cereal, or snacks. Of course, I always paid him back in full. I felt so bad for him. It looked like he put up a struggle, and someone held him down against his will. Someone ran upstairs (I believe it was the brothers Nick or Marcos) to call the cops.

A few minutes later, the police and an ambulance arrived. The investigation was short and quick. They opened up the car and slowly removed his body. The medics had to stretch the victim out. He was bent up as rigor mortis had set in. As they placed the poor guy on the gurney, all I could think about was his family—or did he have a family, kids, a wife? They threw him in the back of the ambulance, and away they went. That was it, a life vanquished. He was only in his midthirties perhaps. But why? I guess I would never know. Tragic ending. RIP.

113. Murder 5, East NY, 1988

In 1988, I started working as a summer youth counselor for the YMCA. It was located on Jamaica Avenue and Shepherd Street. My good friend Big Joe hooked me up with the job. I really enjoyed working at the Y. We played sports, went on outdoor field trips, and enjoyed several other fun recreational activities like swimming. Our supervisor was Julia. She was very stern but very fair and open-minded to many ideas. Our bus driver for outdoor excursions was Julius, a very nice older gentleman who did his best to be patient with unruly kids. Most kids in the program were roughneck youth from some of the toughest neighborhoods around the area, including the housing projects. I had most of them in check. I didn't play when it came down to respect and observing the rules of the program. I didn't put up with any silly nonsense whatsoever. My martial arts background made me well-prepared to deal with intolerance. Don't get me wrong, the kids had tons of fun in the program, but every once in a while, one of them would try to cross the line. That kid was Taekwon. Yes, like Taekwondo. This kid respected no one. He was a shrewd little bastard. He disrespected the staff, the bus driver, the other children, and me. Taekwon was thirteen years old. You'd think he would've had more manners and common sense. Nope! I was eighteen. I tried my best to get through to this knucklehead, but it was fruitless. I kept my cool, but being truthful, deep down inside, all I really wanted to do was to punch him square in the face. Eventually, he was dropped from the program.

One morning, on a beautiful sunny day, we decided to take the kids to the park to get some fresh air. The kids rode the swings, played on the monkey bars and seesaw, and ran through the grassy fields. As we headed back toward the YMCA, a familiar sight caught my eye: yellow tape. Police tape. A perimeter. I looked at Joe and Julia. They both knew exactly what this was: a homicide. The difference now was, it was out in the open, in plain daylight for all the kids to see. As we got closer, we could see the victim. His body was mutilated, and he was burnt beyond recognition. He was riddled with gunshot wounds. Yet something was different about this crime. Something was sticking out of his neck. It was a colombian necktie. The Colombian drug kingpins were known for cutting the throats of their victims and then pulling the victim's tongues through to the other side, thus the necktie. It was the Colombian's mark left upon their victims as a sign of the victim's betrayal and treachery and a warning for others. The ruthless killers dumped the body on the side of the road. It looked like the victim was tortured and murdered elsewhere and then dumped at the park. We tried to shield the kids from seeing the tragedy, but they noticed immediately. One of the very young kids shouted, "Look, another dead body!" I was really disturbed by the comment. The child was only about five years old but was already desensitized to violence and death at such a young age. All the kids saw the body and were nonchalant and relaxed, as if nothing had happened, like it was all routine. I must admit, I, too, felt this way. Just another body, just another day. Yup!

114. Murder 6, Flatbush, 1990

The year was 1990. It was a Friday evening. I was in Flatbush, Brooklyn, training at Shihan (master) Tommy Chen's dojo. The dojo was located on Avenue H. I trained with a friend named Edwin Montanez. Edwin was a B-boy. He was also known as Choco. He was down (a member) with the Masterminds crew in the southside of Brooklyn. We trained till about 11:00 p.m. After our workout, we said our goodbyes and then headed out. We had two ladies with us. As we all made our way to the subway, we decided to take a detour and stop at the pizzeria to get some chow. We were very hungry, and it was a long trip home. After downing (eating) some slices of pizza and some clever conversation, we all proceeded to walk to the subway station near Brooklyn College. That was where the 2 and 5 trains meet. We were exhausted from a good night of exercise and just wanted to get home. We bought our tokens at the booth and then boarded the number 2 train.

It was the dead of winter and very cold out that night. Most straphangers had on coats and jackets. Several passengers wore scarves, gloves, and hats as well. Some dudes rocked (wore) eight-ball jackets while others donned leather trench coats. That evening, the train was packed. Again, it was a Friday night, or, in other words, party night. Luckily for us, we found some empty seats. The train started moving. We passed several stops with no delays whatsoever. It was a good night. *Home sweet home, here I come!* I thought in a relaxed state of mind. That was to be short lived however.

As we approached the Hoyt Street station, we could hear a loud commotion. Bottles were broken. The doors opened, people got off, then others boarded. A young Black gentleman boarded the train and sat down right across from me. He closed his eyes and dozed off. Some women on the platform screamed, "He's on the train! he's on the train!" The doors closed as the train slowly pulled out of the station. Suddenly, the train came to an abrupt halt. It seemed that someone maliciously pulled the emergency cord. We were now stuck halfway between the station and the tunnel. "Those damn kids!" Edwin shouted. I agreed. Kids were always pulling the emergency cords for laughs and thrills back then. All of a sudden, a bunch of thugs started hopping onto the trains from the platform. One by one, they jumped over the chains that separated the train cars. About six of the thugs entered our train car from my left, and about ten of them entered from my right. All of them were young Black teens about sixteen through eighteen years old. A bad moment! It was a chilling situation for us. Something ominous was in the air. Trouble.

It was the Decepticons, better known as the Decept gang. *Shit!* I thought. They borrowed their name from the popular *Transformers* cartoons of the 1980s. The Decepts were a notorious street gang that ravaged New York City with crime and violence in the late 1980s and early 1990s. They were involved in dozens of murders through-out the five boroughs. They were ruthless and were feared for their wilding, which included hundreds of robberies, muggings, stabbings, beatings, and shootings. "Fuck, we're trapped!" I said to myself in a worried tone. I glanced over at my friend Edwin, and he sported a look of deep concern on his face. The thugs started casing the car, sizing potential victims up and down. They stopped right in front of me. One of the thugs had a large gash on his face and was bleeding profusely. He blurted out, "Fuck that, let's rob somebody!" My palms got sweaty. My heart raced. *Who do I hit first, where do I run, and what about the ladies who were with us?* I thought in anticipation of the unfolding event before us. The air was thick like a bomb was about to go off. Passengers scurried off the car into the next one in sheer panic, looking for safety.

One of the thugs noticed a man sleeping across from where I was seated. It was the same young Black gentleman who dozed off a few moments earlier. The thug yelled out, "Yo, that's him!" The Decepticons surrounded the young gentleman. I gasped. I must admit, at that moment, I felt a sense of relief, which in turn later would be a sense of guilt, knowing that the vicious thugs undivided attention was now solely on the gentleman. My line of vision was impaired from all the thugs standing in between the gentleman and myself, but I clearly saw when one of the thugs unleashed a vicious front kick toward the seated gentleman. Another thug threw a punch at the victim, or so I thought. He actually stabbed him in the chest with a knife. All hell broke loose! One of the ladies that accompanied us let out a loud, piercing scream. She kept screaming at the top of her lungs throughout the ordeal. The other passengers made a bee-line for the rear door. Passengers tripped over their own feet in their scurried attempt to escape the lunacy. The train started moving again as all these was unfolding. It was an express train—the express train straight to the bottomless pits of hell.

My biggest worry at that moment was gunfire. Many innocent bystanders were killed by gunshots in the city back then. I surely didn't want to be another statistic. Edwin got up and ran to his left side toward the rear train door, so he could exit into the other car. The train car was now empty except for ourselves, the victim, and the murderous thugs. Everything became eerily silent and slow at that point, even though it happened so quickly. (To this day, my recollection of this tragedy was in slow motion.) As the thugs commenced pouncing on the victim, I turned toward the young lady who kept screaming in shock and firmly grabbed her by the arm and forcefully slung her toward my left side, toward the same direction Edwin ran to. The train bounced as it roared through the tunnel, causing her and Edwin to lose their balance and fall, but they got up and thank-fully made their way into the other car. In the mayhem, the other young lady who accompanied us got separated from our group and ran the other way into the opposite car with several other passengers.

Now, it was just the victim, the gang, and myself in the same car. From the corner of my eye, I could see the lights of the dark tunnel as this train from hell raced through it. We zipped past one station after another, yet the nightmare continued. I looked toward the victim as I made my exit toward the rear door. As I ran to safety in my attempt to escape the violent carnage, I looked over my shoulder and thought side kick to the chest if the thugs tried to attack me, but the beef they had was solely with the victim. Thank God for me, but I felt a deep sense of sadness for the victim. The victim tried in vain to get up and run behind me toward the door. I saw the utter look of terror on the victim's face. He wanted to live so badly. To survive this deadly assault was his only purpose, to exist for another day, but the evil gang was having none of it. The victim tried valiantly to escape in my direction. He was so close to me, less than two feet away, but I couldn't do anything to save him. The attackers had Rambo knives in their hands. The blades alone were about six to eight inches long. One attacker lifted his weapon with a demonic scowl on his face and plunged his knife through the victim's back. It entered the left side of the victim's back and penetrated straight through to the other side. I saw the blade clearly as it exited from the victim's chest. The poor man let out a sigh. Blood from his massive wounds spilled all over me.

The attacker looked possessed. His face was totally distorted, diabolical, and pure evil. The victim shrieked as he was violently stabbed repeatedly by several of the cowards. The devil was at work that night recruiting new souls. I finally exited the car. Many of the passengers in the other car cried hysterically. Several grown men had tears welt up in their eyes. The young female who accompanied us frantically screamed out loud. I yelled at her, "Be quiet!" but it was to no avail. She was attracting undue attention to us. I covered her mouth with my hands, muffling her screams. (Due to mental trauma, she came down with a severe case of agoraphobia and didn't leave her house for a few years after said event.) The victim was still in the first car with the assailants. I peered into the first car through the door window. The victim fell to his knees. The attackers continued their unforgiving, relentless assault by jabbing their knives into the victim's lower spine numerous times. This was an unmanly act of gross cowardice, a deliberate killing by a bunch of spineless fools who didn't or couldn't comprehend the magnitude of their illicit behavior. No compassion was shown to the victim, who crumpled slowly to the floor in a heap of lost effort. I turned away in disgust and anger.

The train finally came to a halt. The conductor yelled out police emergency several times over the loud speaker. I was so angry, pissed off. These lowly bastards executed this poor soul. The attackers ran off in different directions. A few of them whizzed past us in their dire hope to escape persecution for their ungodly predatory and shameful conduct. They were all drenched in the blood of their victim. They ran off the train like a pack of hyenas trying to avoid the wrath of the lion. All the passengers were highly emotional and in a state of shock.

I was the first to slowly reenter the subway car with the victim inside. He was lying on the floor in a pool of blood. I looked down on his face. It seemed like he was staring into space. His eyes were dilated. He was in total shock. His breathing was shallow. I heard a wheezing sound. His body shook uncontrollably. One of his hands held a book bag. His white shirt was now dark red, almost purple from all the blood loss. I could vividly see his stab wounds. There were dozens. He was bleeding out. I looked around, but nobody else came into the car. It was just me and him. A few moments earlier, this gentleman was alive, sitting straight across from me, and now... He looked rather young. I'd say late twenties or early thirties. I felt guilt and anguish. I couldn't do anything to save this man. I felt utterly helpless. The cops were racing to the scene as I exited the car. Edwin and I reunited with the ladies and continued our journey home on another train. I was the closest witness to the murder, and I was traumatized, as so were the others around me. I didn't want to be involved. *Several witnesses could testify*, I thought in distress. The rest of the ride home was grim. No one spoke a word. I had a dead man's blood all over me. I felt ashamed, sorrow. Everyone finally made it to their destinations.

When I arrived home, I peeled off all the bloody layers of clothing and took a long hot shower. After the shower, I threw away the stained clothing into the garbage can. I kept my sneakers, which were soiled with blood. I looked at them for some time while replaying the tragic event over and over again in my head. It was the most gruesome event I ever witnessed. The victim was violently murdered before my eyes in cold blood.

(On the news the next day, it was reported that the young attackers were caught and arrested for their heinous crime. The motive for the crime was a botched robbery. The suspects tried robbing the victim and his friend on the train platform. Several of the suspects had approached the two gentlemen and tried stealing their leather jackets. The friend of the victim pulled out a box cutter and slashed one of the attackers across the face. The friend escaped by jumping into the train tracks and disappearing into the tunnel. The victim got on an arriving train where he met his end at the hands of the criminals. The victim worked at LaGuardia College as a security guard and was coming off work that night. He was married with two young children.)

115. Murder 7, Elmhurst, Queens

While this murder did not take place in Brooklyn, it demonstrated that the streets could be dangerous anywhere in the city. Whether you live in the Bronx, Brooklyn, Queens, or Manhattan, violence could erupt at any time. With a soaring population in the millions, attitudes could flare up. Disagreements and disputes could become hazardous, and occasionally, a life can be extinguished. In a city of this magnitude, it was important to keep your attitude in check. Not always so easy. Whether you were riding the subway, walking the city streets, driving on the expressways, or just hanging out with friends on the block, you must always be vigilant about your surroundings and whom you cross paths with.

One afternoon, I found myself in Elmhurst, Queens. I was teaching a kickboxing class at a local gym. After class, I got a bite to eat at one of the local spots. The area was full of great places to have dinner. A different array of Asian, Indian, and Spanish restaurants was found throughout the coveted area. The aromas swirling about from the variety of divine rotisserie kitchens stirred the appetite, a smorgasbord of rich and tantalizing delicacies from all over the world. After indulging myself in the fine cuisine of one of the establishments, I decided to walk around and check out the shops. I purchased a few things and then decided to head home, for it was getting late. The merchants rolled down their metal security gates after a long day at work. Night was looming, and the local night dwellers usually made their rounds at this time. Street hustlers and vagrants ran amok.

As I walked near Elmhurst Hospital, on my way to the nearest subway station, I came upon a crime scene. It occurred on the door front of a small neighborhood bar. I noticed the police tape right away and knew at that point that it was a homicide. I slowly approached the crime scene and saw a man lying in the doorway. He was motionless, stone-cold dead. His corpse was sadly wedged halfway between the front entrance and the sidewalk. It looked as though the victim tried to make a hasty escape. Inquisitively, I thought, *What was the cause of his demise? Did he have a quarrel with someone inside?* From where I was standing, it looked like he was shot to death. He looked like he was in his early thirties. *Did he have a family?* I wondered. After viewing the police investigation of the crime scene for several minutes, I went home. Tragically, these types of gruesome acts happened often in congested areas such as New York, sometimes due to gang violence or drug disputes gone awry. Another life snuffed in the big city. Yup!

116. Murder 8 and 9, East NY, Murder, Suicide

I was in a cab coming home from work one evening. I was trying to get home as soon as possible so that I could watch a championship boxing fight that was airing on TV. I was accompanied by a friend. The cab driver got on the Jackie Robinson expressway. The car raced through the curvy road. (The expressway used to be called the Interborough Parkway a few years earlier. There were many fatal car wrecks due to head on collisions in the past due to the fact there was no safety divider to separate drivers going in opposite directions. It was rectified with the building of the new and much-improved Jackie Robinson expressway.) As we approached the end of the roadway, I noticed police activity ahead. There were emergency vehicles lined up on the opposite side of the freeway. The cops had their guns drawn. There was a white van parked on the side of the roadway with the driver slumped over the wheel. It looked like there had been an accident of some sort.

The cab made a right turn off the expressway and then made a left turn into Highland Park. He made his way through the park, veering through traffic. I lived a few blocks away. As we made the last turn out of the park, I was taken aback with a scene reminiscent of the first murder I saw in 1985. An NYPD helicopter was buzzing overhead as we approached my building. My whole block was taped off. There were police cars everywhere, and many plain clothes detectives were also on hand. People were lined up on both sides of the street. I heard a woman crying out loud and yelling, "She was like a sister to me! She was like a sister to me!" That was when I noticed the victim lying in the middle of the street. It was a female. Her body was covered by a white sheet. One of her legs was partially exposed. She was wearing high-heeled shoes. The entrance to my building was cordoned off. No one was allowed to leave or enter. People were crying. I asked someone, "Oh my god, what happened?"

He responded, "A man killed his ex-girlfriend and then drove off in a white van." The man continued, "As she came out of the building with several of her friends, the ex-boyfriend exited the van and shot her once at point-blank range with a sawed-off shotgun. She fell face down on the street, and then he shot two more times in the back."

I was appalled. (I've seen several men killed, but this was different. This was the first woman I've seen murdered. It was a case of domestic violence.)

I was worried about my mom. She was home upstairs during the crime. Eventually, the police let the residents who were coming home enter the building. I took the elevator upstairs to check on Mom. She said, "I heard three loud bangs and then loud screaming. I was too frightened to come out." I explained to her what had occurred, and she decided to go downstairs and pray for the victim. Many older women gathered in front of the building. They held hands and prayed together for the soul of the young victim. Perhaps they had daughters and felt great sympathy for the young lady. The victim was lying on the street for quite some time while the detectives canvassed the area, looking for evidence to this horrific scene. One of the NYPD detectives was a female. She dotted down notes on her pad and surveyed the remains of the victim. I could only wonder what was going through her mind and how many other times has she witnessed such atrocities. I personally couldn't believe what I was seeing. It was surreal.

It was getting late, and some of the women were exhausted and wanted to retire and go inside. Two stood behind. One of the older ladies said, "We'll stay here with her. We don't want her to be alone," referring to the victim. I stood a few minutes longer as well.

The other lady said, "She had no family here except for her eight-year-old son. He wasn't home, thank God."

The other woman replied, "She was a very nice person and lived on the fifth floor. She was Dominican."

I lived on the third floor. I remembered seeing the victim ride the elevator with her young son several times. I've also seen her at my gym working out a few times. She was a very quiet person. What a shame! I asked them, "What about her parents?"

They responded, "Her father lives in Florida."

So sad, I thought. (It was reported on the news the next day that the man shot his estranged ex-girlfriend three times and then drove off and shot himself in the head a few blocks away. A murder suicide. The man was the father of the eight-year-old boy. The woman had an order of protection against the father of her child.) Tragic.

117. Latin Freestyle, 1987

Music was always a staple in our house when I was growing up. My parents had a nice collection of all the latest disco, salsa, funk, soul, and rock records, including a wide array of legendary artists like the following: Diana Ross; James Brown, the Jackson 5, Aretha Franklin, Héctor Lavoe, Willie Colón, Celia Cruz, Donna Summer, Barrabas, the Bee Gees, the Rolling Stones, Jefferson Starship, the Beatles, the Eagles, Julio Iglesias, Tony Orlando, the Whispers, the O'Jays, the Supremes, the Temptations, Tom Jones, Elvis Presley, the Whispers, Lou Rawls, Kenny Rogers, the Doobie Brothers, Earth, Wind & Fire, etc. I developed a sense of musicality and creativity during this period of my life (1970s). Like many people, I sang in the shower. I walked city streets singing under my breath. Always a die-hard romantic, I was intrigued by beautiful music and love songs from other great artists and musicians as well, such as Captain & Tennile, Barry Manilow, Shaun Cassidy, Elton John, Marvin Gaye, Smokey Robinson, Billy Joel, Andy Gibb, Lionel Richie, Kool & the Gang, and many, many more. Music from this era was well produced and had great vocals. The harmonies were extremely melodic and beautifully arranged. Being the romantic individual that I was, this music was a perfect fit for me.

For my twelfth birthday in 1982, my parents gave me a used electric organ. I spent countless hours playing on it. The first song I ever wrote on it was called "Unbelievable." I still remember it to this day (forty years later). Hip-hop music came along and rap music on the radio became increasingly popular. The cardboard boxes came out as breakdancing/popping hit the dance scene. Kids were in a frenzy as the new culture exploded into the mainstream market. "Hip-hop you don't stop!" was the slogan of the day. Breaking and popping music was without any doubt heavily influenced by European electro funk. Kraftwerk's "Trans Europe Express" was sampled on several classic hip-hop dance tracks. "Planet Rock," "Play It at Your Own Risk," "Pack Jam," "Electric Kingdom," and other dance hits had this new energy, invoking sound that uplifted dancers into the stratosphere.

By 1986, the breakdance craze had grown cold in NYC. New styles were emerging. Latin freestyle was one these styles. It took its foothold among mostly young Puerto Rican youth. Many Puerto Rican B-boys and B-girls found a new way of expressing themselves through this new medium. Hip-hop gravitated more toward rap and less toward the dancers. Kiss FM and WBLS NYC radio stations still catered toward the rap scene. Eric B. & Rakim, Queen Latifah, Public Enemy, Big Daddy Kane, Run-DMC, Salt-N-Pepa, Boogie Down Productions, UTFO, Biz Markie, Roxanne Shante, Fresh Prince, Marley Marl, MC Shan, and MC Lyte were staples of entertainment on these stations. One station changed directions. Formerly known as 92 KTU, the new format and name of the station became Hot 103. The man behind the new movement was Eddie Rivera (RIP). He created a platform for young, new aspiring artists to showcase their talents. TKA, Cynthia, Judy Torres, George Lamond,

Noel, Coro, Safire, Suave, the Rios Sisters, Corinna, the Nasty Boys, and the Latin Rascals were some of the first and foremost artists to perform in this new genre of music. The new form of music also borrowed a page from the Euro electro sound. The songs were about young love and heartbreaks. Eventually, other ethnicities picked up on the music as well.

On Friday and Saturday nights, I used to throw house parties in East New York, Brooklyn. My friend Jose "Puchy" Rivera from upstairs helped me to promote the party by inviting local teens to the jam. I mixed Electro funk records with freestyle and house. The partygoers loved it. We had so much fun with these get-togethers. Seeing the reaction of the guests at the party, I decided to write my first freestyle song in 1987 called "Broken Hearted." It was a simple little song arranged by my good friend Danny. Danny lived in Bushwick, Brooklyn. He played piano in his church band. He was a kind and very generous person with his time, even though he was busy with a wife and two young children. He always found time for a naive, young aspiring seventeen-year-old crooner. Thank you, Danny, for your generosity.

Soon after, I found myself in a studio owned by Carlos "After Dark" Berrios. It was located in a condo in Rego Park. I reluctantly showed him my amateur demo tape. He gave me some tips and advice that helped me to greatly improve my writing skills. That same night, I met Lissette Melendez. She was working on some tracks for an upcoming album (*Together Forever*). I also met Franc Reyes (*Beat Street*) who did backup vocals for the album. Later on, I decided to form a band called Intrigue. The band included my friend Jimmy who lived upstairs from me in Ozone Park, another friend and pianist Eddie (Lefty) Izquierdo from Astoria, my cousin Paulie from the Bronx, and myself as the lead vocalist. I penned a song called "The Meaning of It All." It was a very up-tempo tune. Our group also had some backup dancers, which included two sisters of whom both attended Franklin K. Lane High School a few years earlier in Brooklyn—Carmen and Elizabeth Garcia and also their friend Gloria. I, too, attended the same school.

We eventually were able to connect with Micmac records producer George Vascones (RIP). He had a studio in the Bronx. It was located on the Grand Concourse near Fordham Road. The studio was called Sparkle Management. We did an audition, and luckily for us, Mr. Vascones really liked the song. He decided to work with us and set us up for a live show with other artists. A very popular radio act known as Rare Arts (Boricua Posse) was present during our audition. They also liked our song and gave us some positive feedback. We were ecstatic. The minute we got back home to Queens, we started rehearsing. The next day, we all went shopping to a couple of stores in Queens Mall. One store was called the Oaktree, and the other one was called Bang Bang. We all bought outfits for the show. We were very excited about performing live, but we had some issues with the backup dancers. We just couldn't see eye to eye on the routines. The show went on without a hitch, but we decided to drop the dancers.

A few months later, we hooked up with a very cool producer named Artie Rodriguez. Artie (the One Man Party) produced several local acts including upcoming young talent Lil Suzy ("Take Me in Your Arms"). One afternoon, the guys and I hopped on a subway and took the F train to Park Slope Brooklyn. Artie had a small studio in his apartment. After introducing ourselves—well, I actually met Artie at a record pool in Manhattan, the New York Record Pool. It was held on Fourteenth Street in a loft near the Meat District. The loft was owned by Eddie Rivera (RIP) of Hot 103 fame. But now getting back to Artie. The guys and I constantly drank hot tea so as to keep our vocals sharp. After warming up, we laid down some tracks. Artie hooked it up with some editing and remixing. He was great. We were very happy and satisfied with the recording. Artie provided us with the TASCAM tape/reel. I went home and blasted the song every day on my home sound system.

A few weeks after, I found myself at Rockaway Beach playing my song on a boom box. A high school buddy named Tommy Colon happened to be nearby and heard the song. He said, "Yo, that song is dope. Can I borrow it. I promise I'll give it back!"

I replied, "Of course, you can," not realizing that I wouldn't see it again. It was my only copy—my mistake for lending it out. Shit happens. Fast-forward into the future, I tried getting some promos for our group Intrigue. Eddie Rivera from the New York Record Pool had just produced a top-selling album with the C+C Music Factory. He also worked with Trilogy. He had tons of experience in the music business and was recognized as the Godfather of Latin Freestyle on the radio waves. He held events every weekend at his loft. Freestyle artists from all over performed on his stage. DJs picked up crates of complimentary new freestyle and house records to play at local parties and clubs. This was a very good marketing tool to introduce the music to the public. I met several cool people at his gatherings, including Ralph "King UpRock" Casanova, who was a widely respected DJ and dancer. We hit it off really well and both were huge Bruce Lee fans. I also met DJ Lino from the Floor Lords breakdance/breaking crew. I witnessed some of the members from his crew perform for the crowd. They just killed it. They were very amazing dancers with extremely graceful moves and acrobatics. They were some of the most top-notch breakers I'd ever seen up to that point.

Unfortunately, by 1991, the music scene was changing, and Latin Freestyle was near its end. Sadly, our group members eventually went their separate ways. I kept DJing with my sound system and mixing Latin Freestyle records just for fun. Yup.

118. Odd Jobs, NYC, Mid-'80s

I had several odd jobs throughout the '80s. Most of them were off the books. As soon as I got my working papers from my school guidance counselor, it was off to work. I had several part-time positions as a teen. I worked in the summertime with an Italian gentleman named Joe who lived across the street from me. We installed home awnings. Joe was a very cool guy who collected classic Mustang cars. Soon after, I worked as a messenger with my friend Skinny Chris. He put in a good word for me with his boss. Chris worked as a clerk in the mail room. I worked as a foot messenger. We worked on Park Row near City Hall. As a messenger, it was my duty to deliver packages from one location to another very quickly. My boss would say, "Anthony, I need this to go uptown to 125th Street, you've got twenty minutes." He'd give me a package and two subway tokens. I would fly out of the mail room top speed heading for the train station. I always made my drops and pickups on time. On Fridays at the end of our shift, we both cashed our measly paychecks. We always went shopping at some local stores. The J&R music shop was one of our favorite spots. We then ended up eating a few burgers at the McDonald's on Wall Street. It was fun times working with Chris.

Later on, I tried getting a job at a health club as an aerobics instructor. I was sixteen at the time. I felt that my martial arts training sufficed for that position, little did I know. I browsed through the yellow pages and skimmed through the *New York Post* and *Daily News*. I eventually ran across a Help Wanted ad for an aerobics instructor. It was in a gym in Park Slope called For Your Body Only. A very polite woman answered the phone. She asked me several questions, and I, of course, answered "yes, yes, yes" to all of them. My uncle once told me if you ever want a job, always tell them you have experience. You could learn on the job. One question she asked me was "Do you have any experience teaching high-impact aerobics?"

I wanted a job really bad, so I lied. "Of course, I have!" I responded.

"Can you come in tomorrow at six a.m. for an audition?" she said.

"No problem!" I shouted back. I woke up at 4:00 a.m. the next day. The gym was on the ass end of Brooklyn. I ate a light breakfast and ran to the Cleveland train station. I hopped on the J train. The ride was an hour long. I was running late. By the time I arrived to the gym, the class was already in session. The class was full of women wearing tight spandex outfits and leotards. I walked in with my gym sweats on. The instructor was in the front and yelled out, "Anthony?" I nodded. She said, "Jump right in!" The class was moving at a frenetic pace. Everyone but me was on beat. When they moved left, I moved right. When they went up, I went down. I tried my best but was totally lost and frustrated. I felt awkward like the character Jack Tripper on the *Three's Company* TV show. In a classic gym episode, he stumbled all over the place in comedic fashion. At the end of class, the aerobics instructor spoke with me. I wasn't yet ready for the teaching position, but she offered me a job at the front desk, which I gladly accepted. My duties were folding towels and attending to the members' needs. I was happy nevertheless. Plus, now, I had free use of the gym.

Sometime later, I got a job in a poster factory. I rolled up posters and stuck them into plastic wrappers, mostly car racing and bikini model posters overall. A few months after, I started working in a restaurant located Yonah Schimel located on East Houston Street in the Lower East Side. It was a German Polish restaurant. They sold potato, cabbage, and spinach knishes, as well as potato and cheese blintzes, moon cookies, apple strudel, and borscht. I washed dishes, mopped floors, and worked on the cash register too. I also ran deliveries to the local market. I usually bought milk that was needed to make the borscht. One afternoon, while making one of my daily runs to the store, I bumped into a local prostitute coming out of the market. She looked like the crackhead version of the pop singer Rick James. She was hideous-looking. She said something under her breath. My poor nostrils flared up. The smell jumped out of her mouth like a madman escaping from the loony bin. Oh man! I almost flipped backward from the dastardly stench. Her stinky breath could melt icebergs. I quickly covered my face to lessen the damage and slithered my way into the store to buy supplies. Whew! I had to catch my breath. She was finally gone. Thank goodness!

My boss Sonny was very cool and fair with his employees. The manager's name was Ahmed. He was from Pakistan. He was very funny but stern with his duties. He made sure all the employees stood on their toes. One day, while I was washing dishes and tidying up the restroom, a commotion took place in front of the restaurant. My boss and a neighborhood crackhead got into a heated exchange. My boss resembled Ralph Kramden from *The Honeymooners* TV show. They both put their dukes up and started fighting on the sidewalk. The punches came in bunches. My boss's huge panda belly bounced up and down during the clash. It was a funny scene, I must admit. The other waiters looked my way and said, "Don't you know karate?" I was like "Yeah, so?" It was over as quickly as it started. My boss dusted himself off as the crackhead took off with the wind on his back. My boss yelled out, "Everyone back to work!" Yup!

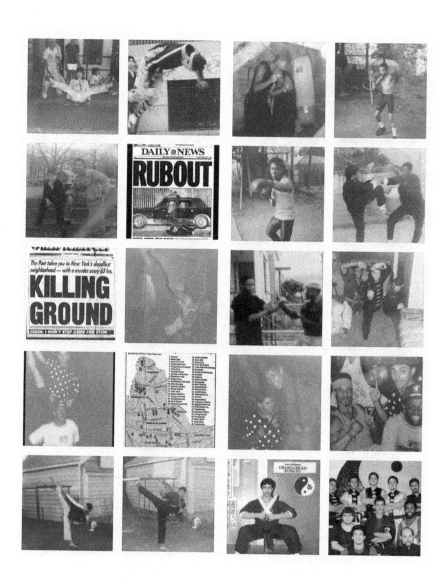

KIDS OF NEW YORK

Courtesy of Richard "Breakeasy" Santiago

Courtesy of Richard "Breakeasy" Santiago

Acknowledgments

I would like to thank everyone and anyone who helped this book become a reality. First, I would like to thank God for giving me the strength to write it. Also my mom and pop, my brother Edward, Irina, my martial arts teachers and associates, all my students at the dojo, Sensei Jose (Tony) Periera, Steven Ponte, Joe English, Mike Matos, Sihing Ricky Velez, Big Luis Castillo, Jose Nunez, Lenny Mosley (RIP), King UpRock, Breakeasy, Joseph Schloss, Kev Ski, Kid Freeze, Errol Thomas, Tony Santiago, John Crudup, Michael Quebec, Sifu Veronica, Richard Richardson, TinyLove, Boogie Bones, EM one, Santiago "Jojo" Torres, DJ Crazy Angelo, DJ Rara, Hector Martinez, George Ruiz, Tommy Chen, Jonas Nunez, Nathan Ingram, Cookie Melendez, Freddy Lopez, Reinaldo Mora, John (Flonetik) Vinuya, Cmar, Jerry Valme, Mighty Mo, Dr. Tom, and Willie Palma. Also, thank you to all my friends and family and the Kids of New York. Thank you, Bruce Lee, for inspiring me to be the best that I could be. Remember, *stay loose*!

About the Author

The author was born in the slums of the South Bronx, New York in 1970. His family moved to Springfield, Massachusetts, at the tender age of three years old. Due to his turbulent home life, his family moved a total of forty-seven times by the time he was fifteen years of age. The author has attended five different public schools in just one year. Due to the influence of the late great Bruce Lee, the author has trained in the martial arts since 1978 and has achieved several black belts in karate and kung fu.

He now teaches at a martial arts school of his own in Queens, New York. The author has produced many black belts throughout the years. He is also the founder of the Kids of New York, an organization that promotes free hip-hop events for youth across the city, which includes competitions in breaking (breakdance) and martial arts. The author's major goal in life is to reach out and change as many lives as possible for the better. The author believes that the most important things in life are family and community. God be with us.

Printed in the USA
CPSIA information can be obtained
at www.ICGtesting.com
LVHW092349051223
765518LV00065B/1250